ARON WARNER'S

# PARIAH

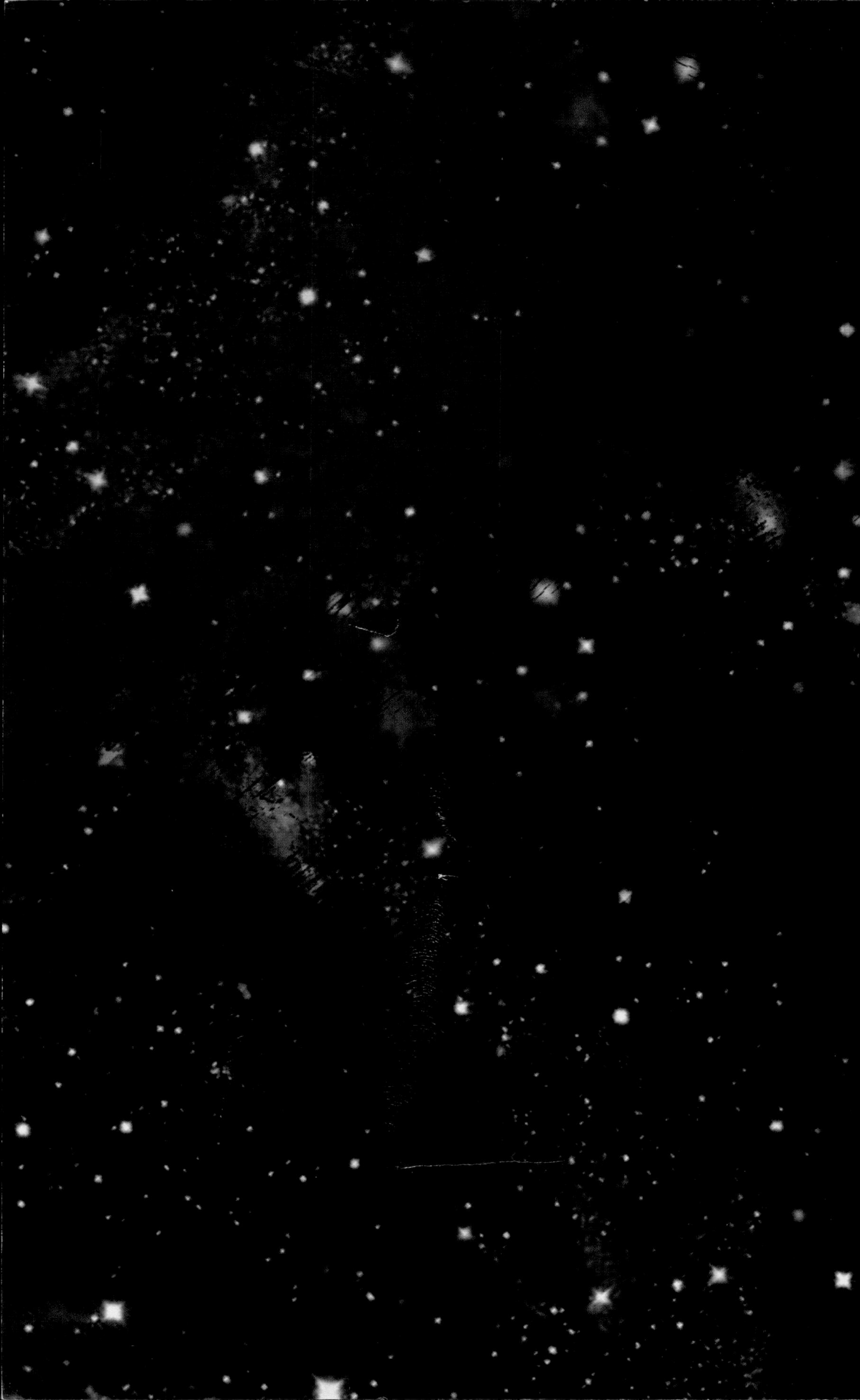

# ARON WARNER'S
# PARIAH
## VOLUME 2

STORY BY
**ARON WARNER** AND **PHILIP GELATT**

ART AND LETTERING BY
**BRETT WELDELE**

COVER AND CHAPTER BREAKS BY
**PAT LEE** AND **BRETT WELDELE**

DARK HORSE BOOKS

EDITOR
**DANIEL CHABON**

ASSISTANT EDITOR
**IAN TUCKER**

DESIGNER
**SANDY TANAKA**

DIGITAL PRODUCTION
**CHRISTINA McKENZIE**

PRESIDENT AND PUBLISHER
**MIKE RICHARDSON**

SPECIAL THANKS TO HANNAH CHECKLEY

EXECUTIVE VICE PRESIDENT NEIL HANKERSON   CHIEF FINANCIAL OFFICER TOM WEDDLE   VICE PRESIDENT OF PUBLISHING RANDY STRADLEY   VICE PRESIDENT OF BOOK TRADE SALES MICHAEL MARTENS   VICE PRESIDENT OF BUSINESS AFFAIRS ANITA NELSON   EDITOR IN CHIEF SCOTT ALLIE VICE PRESIDENT OF MARKETING MATT PARKINSON   VICE PRESIDENT OF PRODUCT DEVELOPMENT DAVID SCROGGY   VICE PRESIDENT OF INFORMATION TECHNOLOGY DALE LAFOUNTAIN SENIOR DIRECTOR OF PRINT, DESIGN, AND PRODUCTION DARLENE VOGEL   GENERAL COUNSEL KEN LIZZI   EDITORIAL DIRECTOR DAVEY ESTRADA   SENIOR BOOKS EDITOR CHRIS WARNER EXECUTIVE EDITOR DIANA SCHUTZ   DIRECTOR OF PRINT AND DEVELOPMENT GARY GRAZZINI ART DIRECTOR LIA RIBACCHI   DIRECTOR OF SCHEDULING CARA NIECE   DIRECTOR OF INTERNATIONAL LICENSING TIM WIESCH   DIRECTOR OF DIGITAL PUBLISHING MARK BERNARDI

PUBLISHED BY DARK HORSE BOOKS
A DIVISION OF DARK HORSE COMICS, INC.
10956 SE MAIN STREET
MILWAUKIE, OR 97222

FIRST EDITION: SEPTEMBER 2014
ISBN 978-1-61655-275-6

1 3 5 7 9 10 8 6 4 2
PRINTED IN CHINA

INTERNATIONAL LICENSING: (503) 905-2377
COMIC SHOP LOCATOR SERVICE: (888) 266-4226

THIS VOLUME COLLECTS *PARIAH* ISSUES #1–#4.

# PARIAH VOLUME 2

# CHAPTER ONE

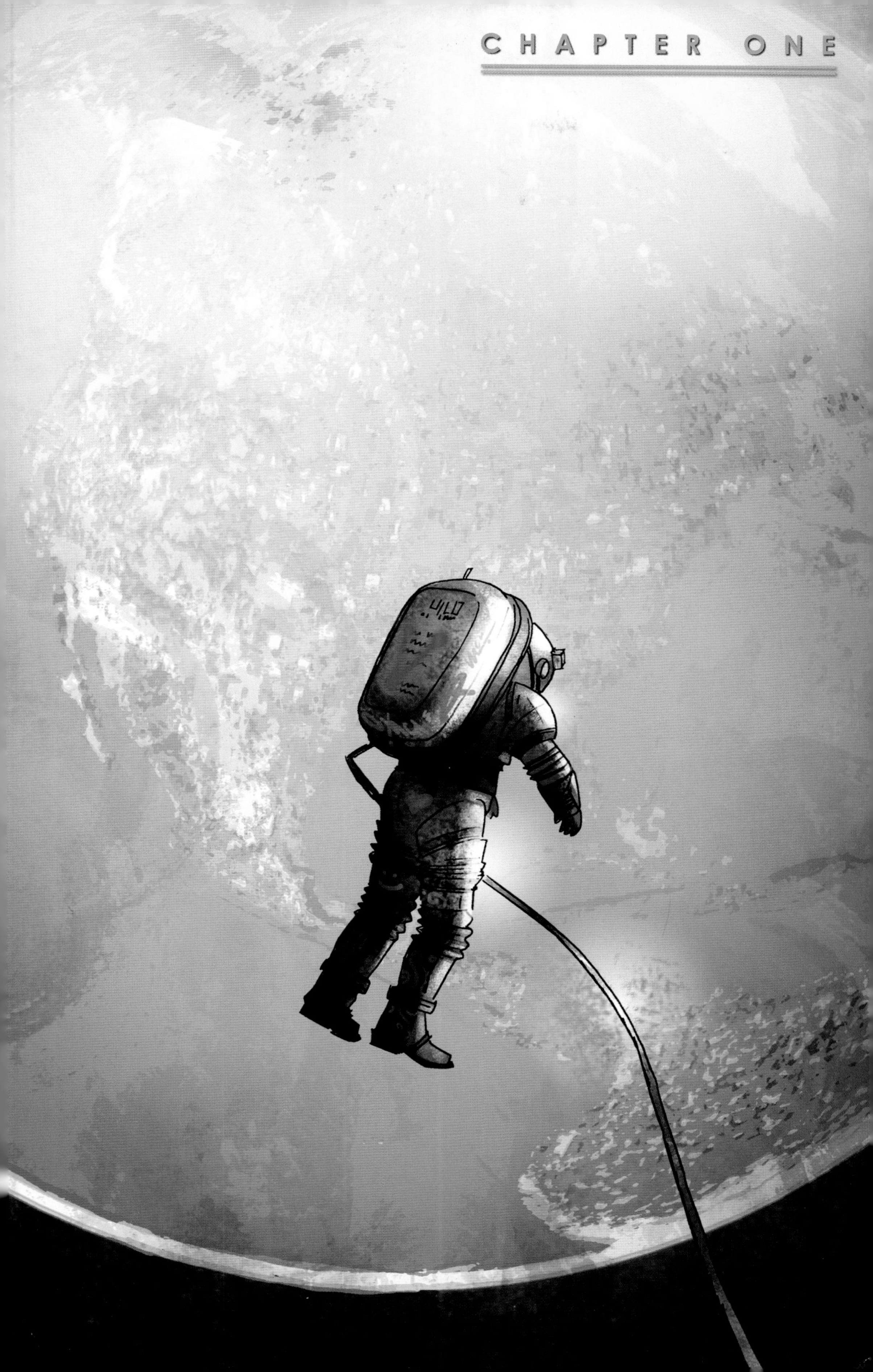

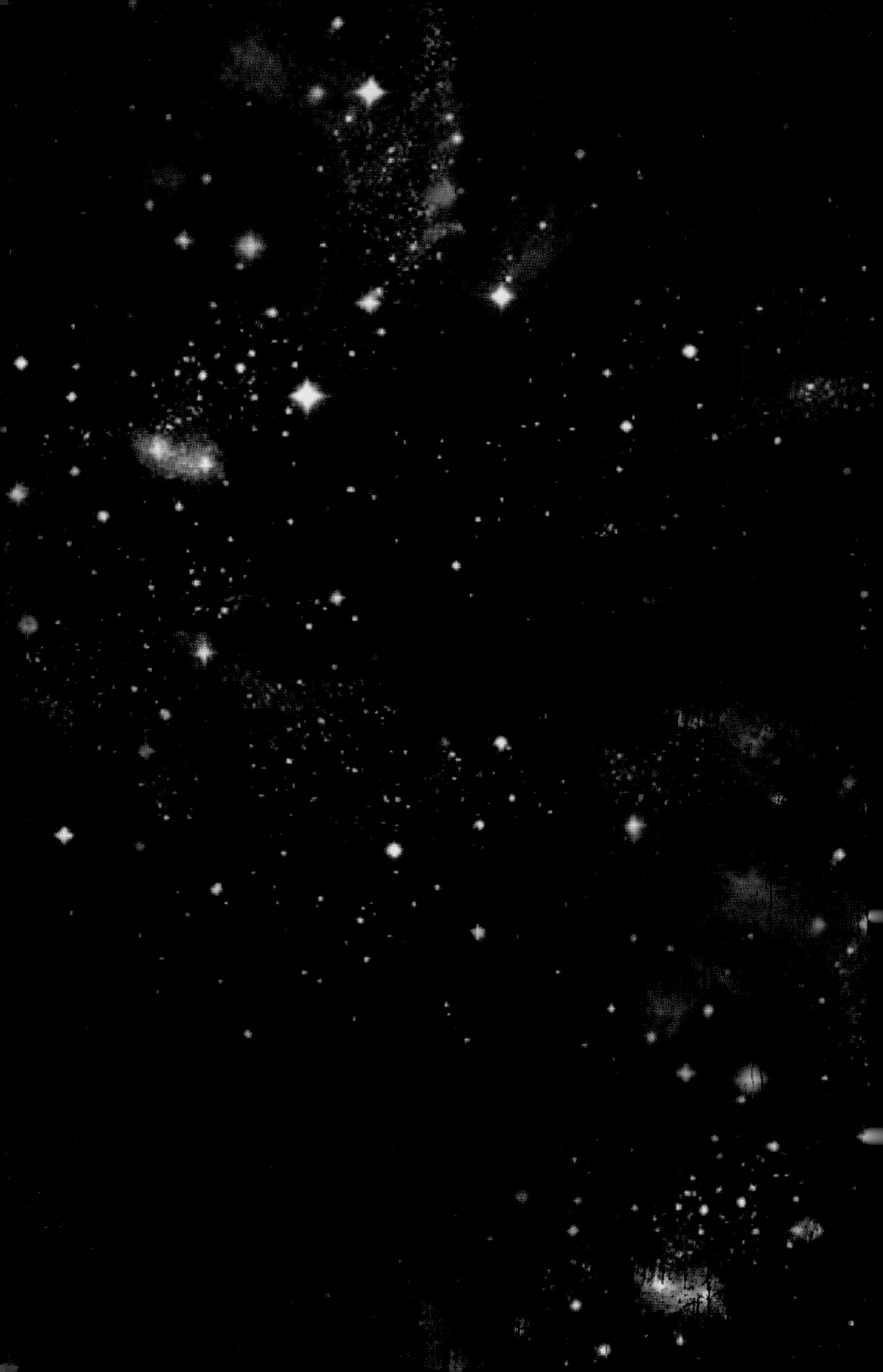

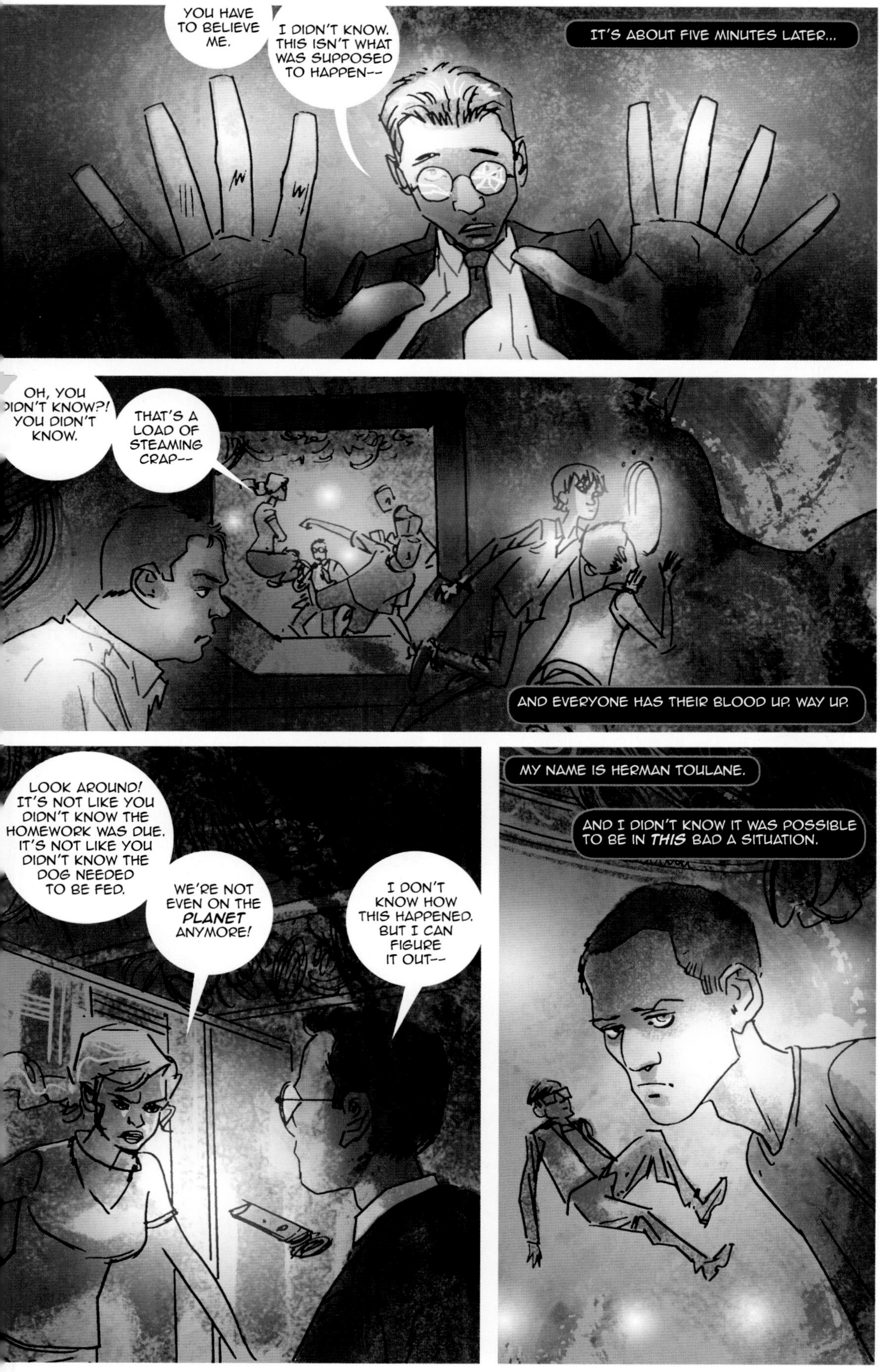

YOU HAVE TO BELIEVE ME.
I DIDN'T KNOW. THIS ISN'T WHAT WAS SUPPOSED TO HAPPEN--
IT'S ABOUT FIVE MINUTES LATER...
OH, YOU DIDN'T KNOW?! YOU DIDN'T KNOW.
THAT'S A LOAD OF STEAMING CRAP--
AND EVERYONE HAS THEIR BLOOD UP. WAY UP.
LOOK AROUND! IT'S NOT LIKE YOU DIDN'T KNOW THE HOMEWORK WAS DUE. IT'S NOT LIKE YOU DIDN'T KNOW THE DOG NEEDED TO BE FED.
WE'RE NOT EVEN ON THE *PLANET* ANYMORE!
I DON'T KNOW HOW THIS HAPPENED. BUT I CAN FIGURE IT OUT--
MY NAME IS HERMAN TOULANE.
AND I DIDN'T KNOW IT WAS POSSIBLE TO BE IN *THIS* BAD A SITUATION.

YOU OKAY, TOULANE?

YEAH, YEAH, I'M FINE. CAN'T SAY AS MUCH FOR EVERYONE ELSE THOUGH--

SO I MIGHT NEVER SEE EARTH AGAIN. THERE'S THAT. BUT I'M FINE WITH THAT.

...I THINK...

HELL, WHEN THEY STARTED ROUNDING VITROS UP, I GAVE MYSELF UP VOLUNTARILY.

SO LOOK, I KNOW YOU HAVE THIS IDEA THAT YOU'RE, LIKE, OUR LEADER OR SOMETHING--

I NEVER CLAIMED I WAS--

IF YOU'D SPENT EVEN A SINGLE NIGHT IN MY HOUSE, WITH MY MOTHER AND *DAN*, MY STEPDAD, WELL...

YOU'D HAVE DONE THE SAME. TURNING MYSELF IN SEEMED LIKE A TICKET OUT.

BUT ALL THAT IS OVER NOW. WE'RE GOING TO FIND A NICE PLACE TO STUFF YOU FOR NOW, HYDE.

YEAH, WE'RE GOING TO DO THAT. BUT WE'R GOING TO DO THAT...WITHOUT YOU.

THE VITROS WERE SUPPOSED TO BE MY NEW FAMILY. MY REAL FAMILY.

I KNOW WHAT YOU'RE THINKING: "SO NAIVE."

YOU'D BE RIGHT TO THINK IT.

THE TWO FAMILIES FEEL PRETTY INTERCHANGEABLE RIGHT NOW.

LET ME GO!

THIS ISN'T GOING TO END WELL.

Y'THINK?

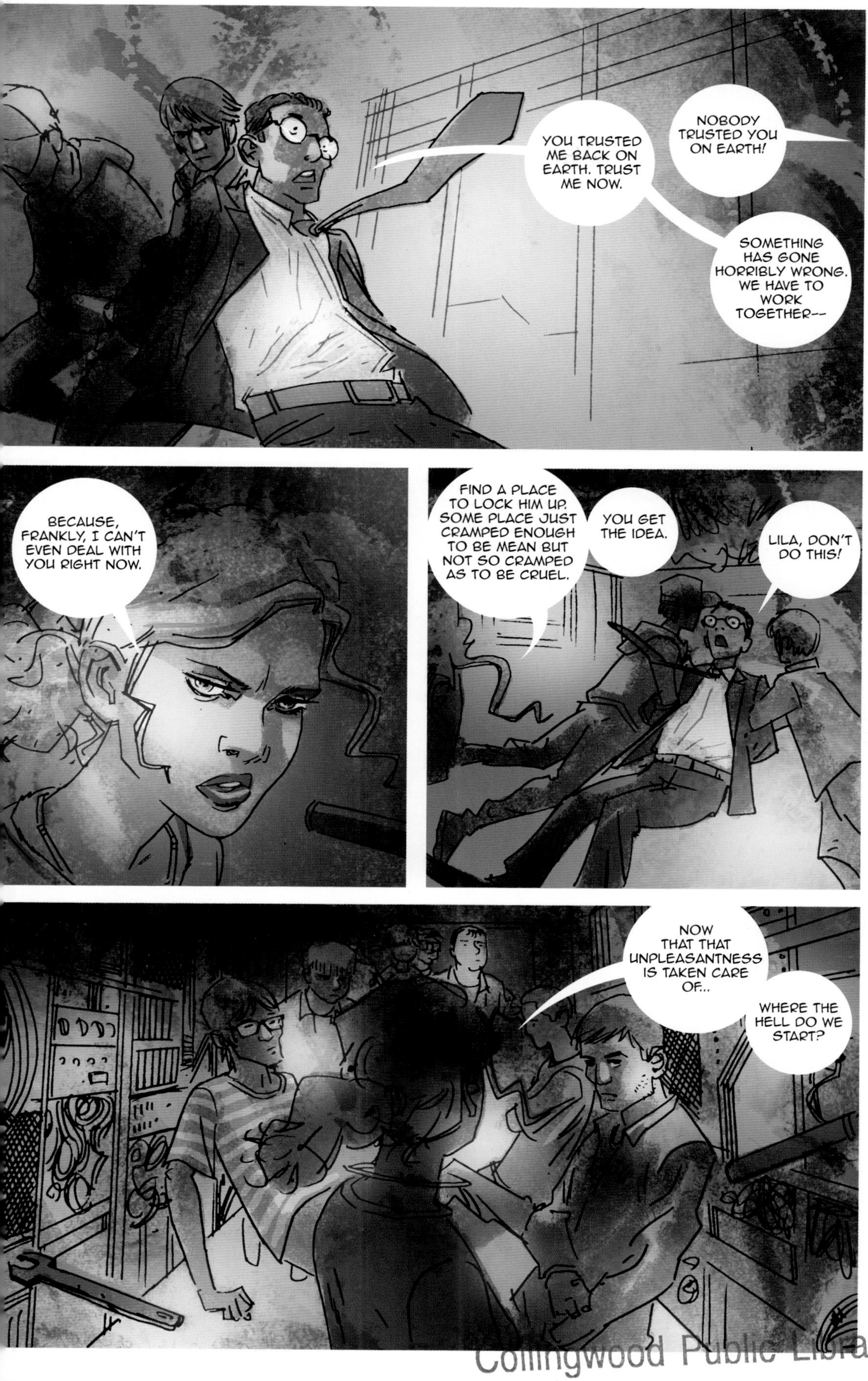
YOU TRUSTED ME BACK ON EARTH. TRUST ME NOW.
NOBODY TRUSTED YOU ON EARTH!
SOMETHING HAS GONE HORRIBLY WRONG. WE HAVE TO WORK TOGETHER--
BECAUSE, FRANKLY, I CAN'T EVEN DEAL WITH YOU RIGHT NOW.
FIND A PLACE TO LOCK HIM UP. SOME PLACE JUST CRAMPED ENOUGH TO BE MEAN BUT NOT SO CRAMPED AS TO BE CRUEL.
YOU GET THE IDEA.
LILA, DON'T DO THIS!
NOW THAT THAT UNPLEASANTNESS IS TAKEN CARE OF...
WHERE THE HELL DO WE START?

LILA PUTS MARKS IN CHARGE OF ENGINEERING.

HE BRINGS ME ALONG AS A SECOND IN COMMAND.

ABOUT AN HOUR LATER, WE HAVE A VERY SCIENTIFIC, THOROUGH, AND IN-DEPTH ASSESSMENT OF OUR SITUATION.

WE'RE SCREWED.

IT COULD BE WORSE.

YEAH, I GUESS WE COULD ALREADY BE DEAD.

THIS IS A SCHEMATIC OF THE ENTIRE PLACE. IT'S BIG, IT'S COMPLICATED, AND IT'S HARD TO TELL WHAT IS WHAT. A LOT OF THE SYSTEMS ARE RUNNING ON AN AUTOPILOT SET UP BEFORE MOST OF US WERE BORN.

IT'S ALL OLD. THE ENTIRE STATION. THE LIFESPAN OF A PLACE LIKE THIS IS... SHORT. AND THESE ARE OUR PROBLEMS, LISTED IN NO PARTICULAR ORDER, SINCE THEY'RE ALL BIG ONES:

$CO_2$ SCRUBBERS ARE INEFFICIENT TO THE POINT OF USELESSNESS; WE ARE LOSING $O_2$ LEVELS EVERY DAY WE'RE UP HERE; FOOD SUPPLIES ARE TINY AND FOOD-CREATION OPTIONS ARE MINIMAL AT BEST; WE HAVE NO WAY TO PROPERLY GENERATE ELECTRICITY... AND OUR "FUEL" SOURCE IS ARCHAIC.

AND THAT DOESN'T EVEN GET US INTO THE CREATURE COMFOR--

ALL RIGHT, ALL RIGHT!

I GET IT. THERE ARE PROBLEMS.

LET'S TALK ABOUT WHAT WE WANT. CAN THIS THING GET US BACK TO EARTH?

IT IS COMMON KNOWLEDGE THAT LILA ISN'T KNOWN FOR HER PATIENCE OR POISE. I CAN CONFIRM THAT--

IT CERTAINLY WASN'T MEANT TO DO ANYTHING LIKE THAT--

BUT MAYBE, POSSIBLY, EVENTUALLY, WITH MONUMENTAL AMOUNTS OF WORK...WE COULD REENTER ORBIT AND LAND IT. AND MAYBE ALL SURVIVE.

LET MARKS HANDLE HER.

BUT THE LIFE SUPPORT AND OTHER PROBLEMS NEED TO BE FIXED FIRST, BEFORE WE START TALKING BIG-TIME PLANS.

FINE. BUT I WANT TO GET BACK ON EARTH. I THINK WE ALL WANT TO GET BACK ON EARTH, AS SOON AS POSSIBLE.

THAT'S THE MOMENT I KNOW THAT LILA AND I WILL NEVER SEE EYE TO EYE ON THINGS. I DO NOT THINK WE BELONG ON EARTH.

LET'S STABILIZE OURSELVES UP HERE AND THEN WE CAN WORK ON GETTING HOME.

GREAT. I'LL BE BACK IN A BIT TO CHECK ON YOU BOYS.

TWO HOURS LATER AND THE AIR IS SO THICK WITH TENSION THAT I CAN BARELY BREATHE.

OR IT MIGHT JUST BE THAT THE AIR PUMPING THROUGH HERE IS THAT STALE.

WHATEVER THE CASE, IT IS AWFUL.

LOOK, I'M SCARED TOO, OKAY? IT'S OKAY TO BE SCARED.

I'M NOT SCARED. I'M PISSED OFF!

YEAH, BELIEVE ME, I'M WAY MORE THAN PISSED OFF.

BUT WE CAN'T START GETTING THINGS DONE UNLESS WE HAVE A REALLY STRONG CENTRAL VOICE. I CAN LEAD US.

LILA WANTS TO BE THE LEADER.

I THINK THAT'S A TERRIBLE IDEA.

I ALSO THINK THIS IS ALL ON THE CUSP OF GOING COMPLETELY TITS UP.

LOOK, I THINK YOU'D BE A GREAT LEADER FOR US, BUT YOU CAN'T JUST PROCLAIM YOURSELF TO BE ONE.

WE SHOULD VOTE FOR A LEADER--

RIGHT NOW THE VITRO SOCIAL SYSTEM IS ON A CRASH COURSE WITH DISASTER.

C'MON, THIS ISN'T 1776. WE'RE TRAPPED... ON A SPACE STATION...ORBITING A HOSTILE EARTH...

RELYING ON DEMOCRACY IN A CRISIS LIKE THIS IS LIKE RELYING ON AN ARGYLE SWEATER IN A NUCLEAR WINTER.

WE ARE IN SPACE RIGHT NOW. IN. SPACE. AND INSTEAD OF FIGURING OUT WHAT TO DO ABOUT THAT, WE'RE ARGUING ABOUT POLITICS OR SOME CRAP.

IS OUR INTELLIGENCE GETTING IN THE WAY? IS IT RUINING THIS FOR US?

# AUTOMATED ORBITAL CORRECTION INITIATED. PREPARE FOR BURN.

I HEARD ONCE THAT ALL SYSTEMS DETERIORATE, THAT ALL THINGS TREND TOWARDS CHAOS. I CAN'T REMEMBER WHERE I HEARD IT AND I REMEMBER THINKING THE SPEAKER WAS BEING A TAD BOMBASTIC.

BUT MAYBE THAT *IS* JUST THE WAY OF IT.

AND MAYBE THE VITROS ARE NO DIFFERENT.

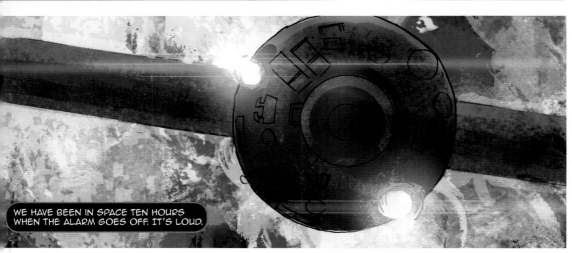

WE HAVE BEEN IN SPACE TEN HOURS WHEN THE ALARM GOES OFF. IT'S LOUD.

SQUEEEEEEEEEE

THE PROBLEM IS PRETTY IMMEDIATELY CLEAR. SO AT LEAST WE DON'T HAVE TO SORT IT OUT.

A ROUTINE BURN OF THE PRIMARY THRUSTERS WAS SUPPOSED TO KEEP US IN ORBIT. INSTEAD IT HAS SENT US HURTLING BACK TOWARDS EARTH.

DESPITE LILA'S EARLIER HOPE FOR US TO ONE DAY FLY BACK TO EARTH, SHE'S NOT EXCITED BY THIS NEWS.

WHAT THE HELL IS GOING ON!

THE STATION'S ORBIT IS RAPIDLY DETERIORATING...

JUST TELL ME YOU CAN FIX IT, FAST.

IT'S NOT THAT SIMPLE. THE SYSTEM HAS LOCKED UP ON US. WE HAVE NO CONTROL.

THIS THING JUST WENT FROM A SPACE STATION TO A DEATH TRAP.

BY MY CALCULATION, WE'RE GOING TO GAIN ABOUT FIVE DEGREES OF TEMPERATURE PER HOUR.

WE'LL ALL BE BOILED ALIVE IN UNDER FIVE HOURS.

N HOUR LATER AND WE'VE ESTABLISHED HAT THE CODING IS HOPELESS.

A LOST CAUSE.

88.9° F

IT'S MY IDEA TO CRACK THE SYSTEM OPEN AND CLIMB INSIDE OF IT, LITERALLY.

WHAT IF I'M CLAUSTROPHOBIC AND DIDN'T KNOW IT?

WE NEED BOARD D20 FROM THE BACK QUADRANT. IT'S THE OVERSEER PIECE FOR THE WHOLE THRUSTER OPERATION--

CRAP.

YOU KNOW THAT GAME, THAT KIDS' GAME, "WHICH ONE OF THESE THINGS DOESN'T BELONG?"

YEAH, ONE OF THESE DOESN'T BELONG.

BOARD D20 LOOKS ABOUT TEN YEARS NEWER THAN ANYTHING ELSE IN HERE. IN FACT, IT LOOKS BRAND NEW.

I'M COMING OUT. WE HAVE A PROBLEM.

THINGS SUDDENLY COME A SMIDGE MORE INTO FOCUS FOR ME.

THE WHOLE SHIP IS OUTDATED. OLD. DYING. EXCEPT THIS.

THIS WAS PUT IN JUST BEFORE WE GOT HERE. IT'S THE TRAJECTORY BOARD. AND IT'S HEAVILY ENCRYPTED. AND THERE ARE PROBABLY COUNTLESS OTHERS SPREAD THROUGH THE SYSTEM.

WHOEVER SENT US UP HERE, WHOEVER PREPPED THIS PLACE FOR US, THEY SET IT UP SO THAT THIS STATION WOULD FAIL.

THIS PLACE IS MEANT TO KILL US AND MAKE IT LOOK LIKE AN ACCIDENT.

A CONVENIENT WAY TO GET RID OF AN INCONVENIENT PROBLEM.

IN A SENSE, I FEEL FLATTERED. THAT'S A LOT OF WORK JUST TO GET RID OF US.

I DON'T THINK IT'S TIME FOR JOKING, LILA.

LOVERS' QUARRELS. AS IF I HADN'T SEEN ENOUG OF THOSE IN MY DAYS.

I KNOW THAT, BRANDON. HEY, SOMETIMES YOU HAVE TO SMILE AT HOW ABSURD ALL OF THIS IS--

NEVER MIND.

CAN YO FIX IT?

DEPENDS WHAT YOU MEAN BY "IT" AT THIS POINT.

DON'T, MARKS, I'M NOT IN THE MOOD.

CAN YOU KEEP US ALIVE?

WE WON'T BE ABLE TO FIX THE SYSTEM AS IT IS, NOT IN THE TIME WE HAVE LEFT.

THAT IS THE HARD TRUTH. SOMETIMES THE NUMBERS ARE NOT IN YOUR FAVOR.

SO WHAT? WE'RE ALREADY DEAD?

NO. THE SYSTEMS CURRENTLY IN PLACE *ARE* USELESS TO US BUT--

BUT WE HAVE TIME TO MAKE OUR OWN SYSTEM.

IT MIGHT NOT BE PRETTY. BUT WE'RE VITROS. AND WE CAN GOD DAMNED WELL DO IT.

MARKS AND I MAKE THE PLAN.

IT'S NOT PRETTY. IT'S DANGEROUS AND DIRTY AND WE HAVE ONLY HOURS TO EXECUTE IT.

I BET ANY ROCKET SCIENTIST ON EARTH WOULD FLAT OUT CALL IT CRAZY.

BUT SCREW IT. NEVER SAY DIE, RIGHT?

98.4.

IN THE LOWER DECKS OF THE SHIP WHERE THE LIGHTS DON'T WORK AND THE OXYGEN IS THIN. IT DOESN'T CREAK LIKE AN OLD SAILING SHIP...BUT FOR A MOMENT I FANTASIZE THAT IT IS.

THEN I REALIZE...I'VE NEVER BEEN ON AN OCEAN. IS THAT WEIRD?

ACCORDING TO THE LAST STORAGE MANIFEST, WHICH WAS, BY THE WAY, ALL IN RUSSIAN...

DON'T BRAG.

SORRY... SOMEWHERE DOWN HERE IS THE STORE OF HYDRAZINE.

WE CAN HEAR HYDE. LILA'S ENFORCERS LOCKED HIM BACK THERE.

WHAT IS GOING ON? IT GETTING REAL HOT IN HERE. LET ME HELP!

BUT THERE IS NO TIME NOW TO DEAL WITH THAT SITUATION.

GOT IT.

HYDRAZINE IS A HIGHLY VOLATILE, HIGHLY ARCHAIC ROCKET FUEL. IT IS TO CUTTING-EDGE PROPULSION WHAT MULES WERE TO A V-8 ENGINE.

BUT SOMETIMES INSTABILITY IS A PLUS. WE'RE GOING TO USE THE EXTRA STORE OF IT TO CAUSE A CONTROLLED EXPLOSION...

WARNING
DANGEROUS CONTENTS
HANDLE WITH EXTREME CARE
НЕ ВЛЕЗАЙ
УБЬЕ-1
СГМ,
ОПАСНО
ДЛЯ ЖИЗНИ

...AND BLOW OURSELVES BACK INTO ORBIT.

WARNING
DANGEROUS CONTENT
HANDLE WITH EXTREME CA
НЕ ВЛЕЗАЙ
УБЬЕ-1
СГ?
ВЛАСТ
ДЛЯ ЖИ

WITH THE EXPLOSIVES LOCATED, WE MOVE ON TO THE BIGGER PROBLEM...

THE MATH.

**100.1·**

IF WE ARE OFF BY AN INCH IN WHERE WE PLANT THE EXPLOSIVES, IF WE MISCALCULATE HOW MUCH WE NEED BY EVEN A MILLIGRAM, IF WE ARE OFF IN ANYTHING BY EVEN THE SLIGHTEST... WE ARE DEAD.

THERE ARE CERTAIN VITROS WHO ARE INTELLIGENT TO THE POINT WHERE THEY SEEM...OFF.

SAM IS ONE OF THEM. BEHIND HER ARE ALL THE OTHERS. THE HUMAN COMPUTERS...75% COMPUTER. 25% HUMAN.

HI.

THEY FREAK ME OUT A BIT.

IN A SENSE, SIMPLE.

THIS ISN'T REALLY ROCKET SCIENCE. IT'S ROCKET SCIENCE WITHOUT THE ROCKET.

IT'S EXPLOSION SCIENCE. WITH ABOUT ONE THOUSAND, TWO HUNDRED FIFTY-FIVE TO THE TENTH POWER VARIABLES.

PLUS ACCOUNTING FOR UNFORESEEN VARIABLES. IT IS DELICATE WORK.

BUT WE WILL DO IT.

RIGHT.

THEY'LL WORK ON CALCULATING THE MATH BEHIND THE EXPLOSION WHILE WE GET A SUPPLY OF THE HYDRAZINE OUT TO THE PROPER QUADRANT--

I HAVE A QUESTION. WHAT EXACTLY DO YOU MEAN BY "OUT"...?

OUR NEXT PROBLEM. THE EXPLOSIVES NEED TO BE STRAPPED TO THE EXTERIOR OF THE STATION.

AND THESE ARE THE ONLY SPACE SUITS AVAILABLE.

LIKE EVERYTHING IN THIS PLACE, THESE THINGS ARE ANCIENT BY MODERN STANDARDS.

BUT THEY DO SEEM TO FUNCTION.

UNFORTUNATELY THEY ARE FIT RELIANT. AND NONE OF US IS GOING TO FIT THESE THINGS.

THE WAY I SEE IT, WE HAVE A FEW OPTIONS.

BUT ALL OF THEM CUT INTO AN ALREADY TIGHT TIME FRAME AND I DON'T LIKE ANY OF THEM--

I HAVE A PLAN.

IT'LL FIT ME.

I'LL MAKE IT FIT ME.

BRENT TAKES ABOUT A MINUTE TO TRY TO CONVINCE ME NOT TO.

WE BOTH KNOW THIS IS THE ONLY WAY TO MAKE THIS THING WORK.

SO, I'VE NEVER BEEN ON A SPACE WALK BEFORE. SO WHAT.

WE'RE ALL HAVING A LOT OF FIRST EXPERIENCES THIS WEEK.

I HOPE I DON'T SWEAT THROUGH THIS THING. PIT STAINS ON A SPACE SUIT, IS THAT POSSIBLE?

I DIDN'T KNOW I COULD SWEAT THIS MUCH.

I DIDN'T *WANT* TO KNOW I COULD SWEAT THIS MUCH.

105. F

THIS IS THE MOST UNCOMFORTABLE I'VE EVER BEEN.

HOW'S THAT?

COULD BE WORSE.

...ACTUALLY NO. IT PROBABLY COULDN'T BE WORSE.

THANKS.

EACH POUCH HAS FOUR MILLIGRAMS OF HYDRAZINE.

THIS PACK HERE HAS THE STICKY IN IT.

WHEN WE KNOW HOW MUCH AND WHERE, WE'LL TELL YOU.

SAM ASSURED ME IT WON'T BE LONG.

BUT I CAN'T TELL IF THEY EVEN UNDERSTAND TIME THE WAY WE DO.

AND HOW MUCH TIME DO WE HAVE?

NOT MUCH. YOU HAVE TO MOVE AS FAST AS YOU CAN ONCE YOU'RE OUT.

BEGINNING EGRESS IN T-MINUS 10...

...9...

PRESSURE IS 12 KPA.

...6...

...5...

HATCH IS NOW LIVE.

...3...

...2...

...1.

THE FEAR TRIPS AWAY.

AND AWAY I GO, TRIPPIN OUT INTO THE VOID.

I HAVE AN ABSURD THOUGHT: "DON'T LOOK DOWN."

I DON'T KNOW WHAT IT IS BUT I ALMOST START LAUGHING.

IF YOU HAD SAID TO ME, "YOU MIGHT DIE," RIGHT THEN...

I WOULD HAVE SAID, "SO WHAT."

I'M ON MY WAY.

SHOULD BE ONLY THIRTY FEET BACK ALONG THE HULL--

YIKES.

WOW.

THAT'S WHERE I'M HEADING.

WE'RE STILL WORKING IN HERE.

GETTING CLOSER.

LAST TIME I CHECKED, "CLOSE" ISN'T THE SAME AS "THERE."

LILA, DO NOT PLAY SEMANTIC GAMES WITH ME.

IF WE ARE WRONG, WE ALL DIE. IF THAT IS WHAT YOU PREFER, WE CAN HAVE HIM PLACE THE EXPLOSIVES RIGHT NOW.

EVEN UP HERE. ECHOES OF MY PARENTS' DIVORCE.

SAMANTHA IS RIGHT, OF COURSE.

IT'S GOING TO BE A LITTLE BIT LONGER.

I'M SORRY, HERMAN.

EVERYONE KNOWS WHAT'S HAPPENED.

I DON'T HAVE ENOUGH TIME TO PLACE THE EXPLOSIVES AND GET BACK INTO THE SHIP.

I KNOW. I AM READY WHENEVER THEY ARE.

IT'S FUNNY.

THE MOMENT I *KNOW* I'M GOING TO DIE OUT HERE, I STILL HAVE THE SAME THOUGHT: "SO WHAT."

TOOK ME TEN MINUTES TO GET OUT HERE. IT'LL TAKE ME TEN MINUTES TO GET BACK, AT LEAST. THE HEAT LEVELS ARE TOO HIGH.

SOMETIMES THE MATH JUST ISN'T ON YOUR SIDE.

BUT IF YOU'RE LUCKY, YOU CAN STILL ACCOMPLISH WHAT NEEDS TO BE ACCOMPLISHED.

AND IT IS BEAUTIFUL OUT HERE.

WE HAVE THE QUADRANT AND DOSAGE!

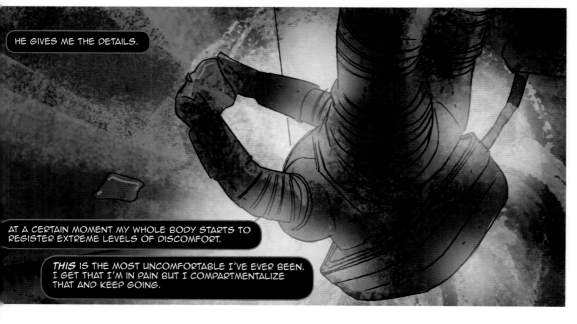

HE GIVES ME THE DETAILS.

AT A CERTAIN MOMENT MY WHOLE BODY STARTS TO REGISTER EXTREME LEVELS OF DISCOMFORT.

*THIS* IS THE MOST UNCOMFORTABLE I'VE EVER BEEN. I GET THAT I'M IN PAIN BUT I COMPARTMENTALIZE THAT AND KEEP GOING.

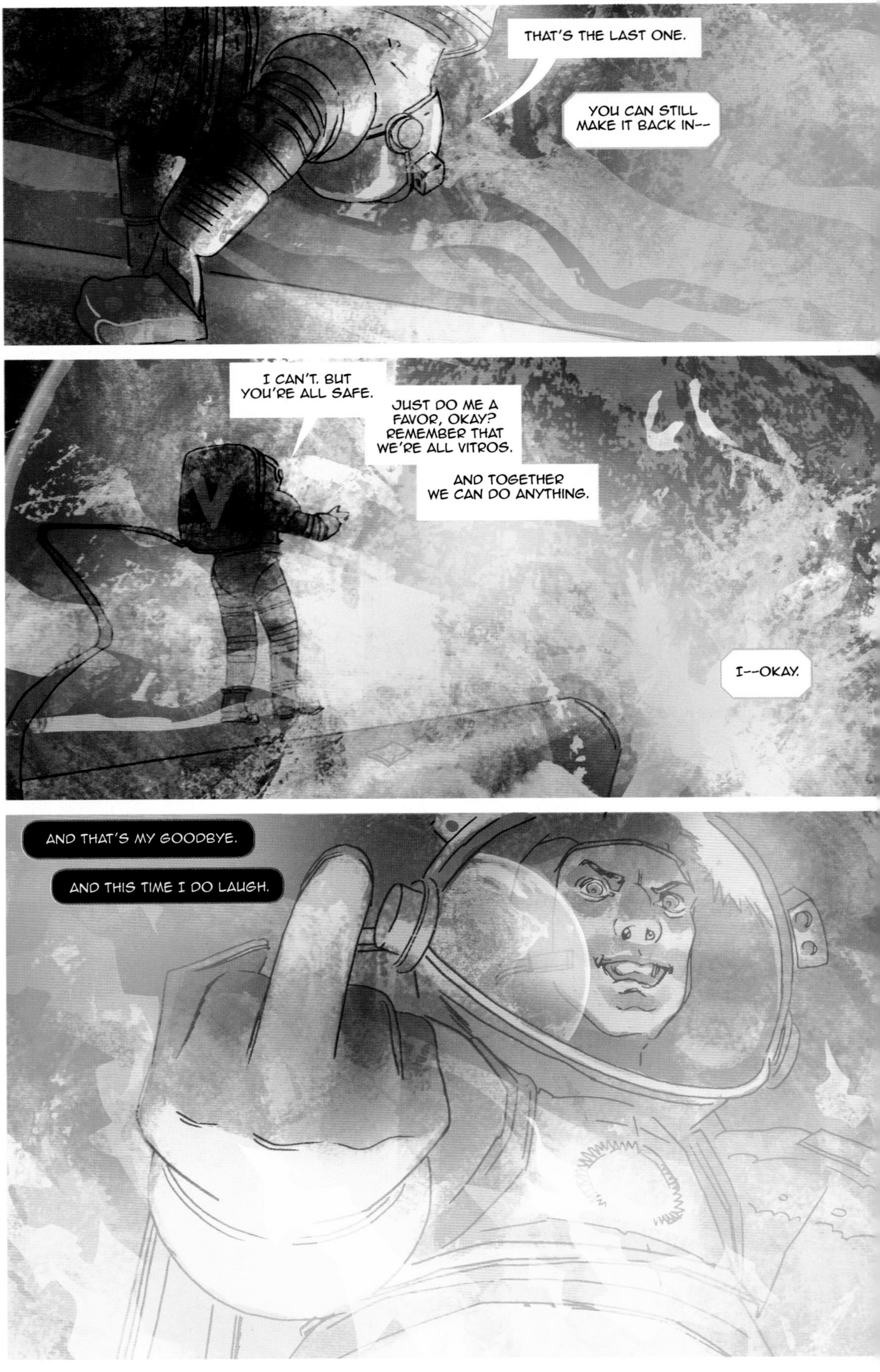
THAT'S THE LAST ONE.
YOU CAN STILL MAKE IT BACK IN--
I CAN'T. BUT YOU'RE ALL SAFE.
JUST DO ME A FAVOR, OKAY? REMEMBER THAT WE'RE ALL VITROS.
AND TOGETHER WE CAN DO ANYTHING.
I--OKAY.
AND THAT'S MY GOODBYE.
AND THIS TIME I DO LAUGH.

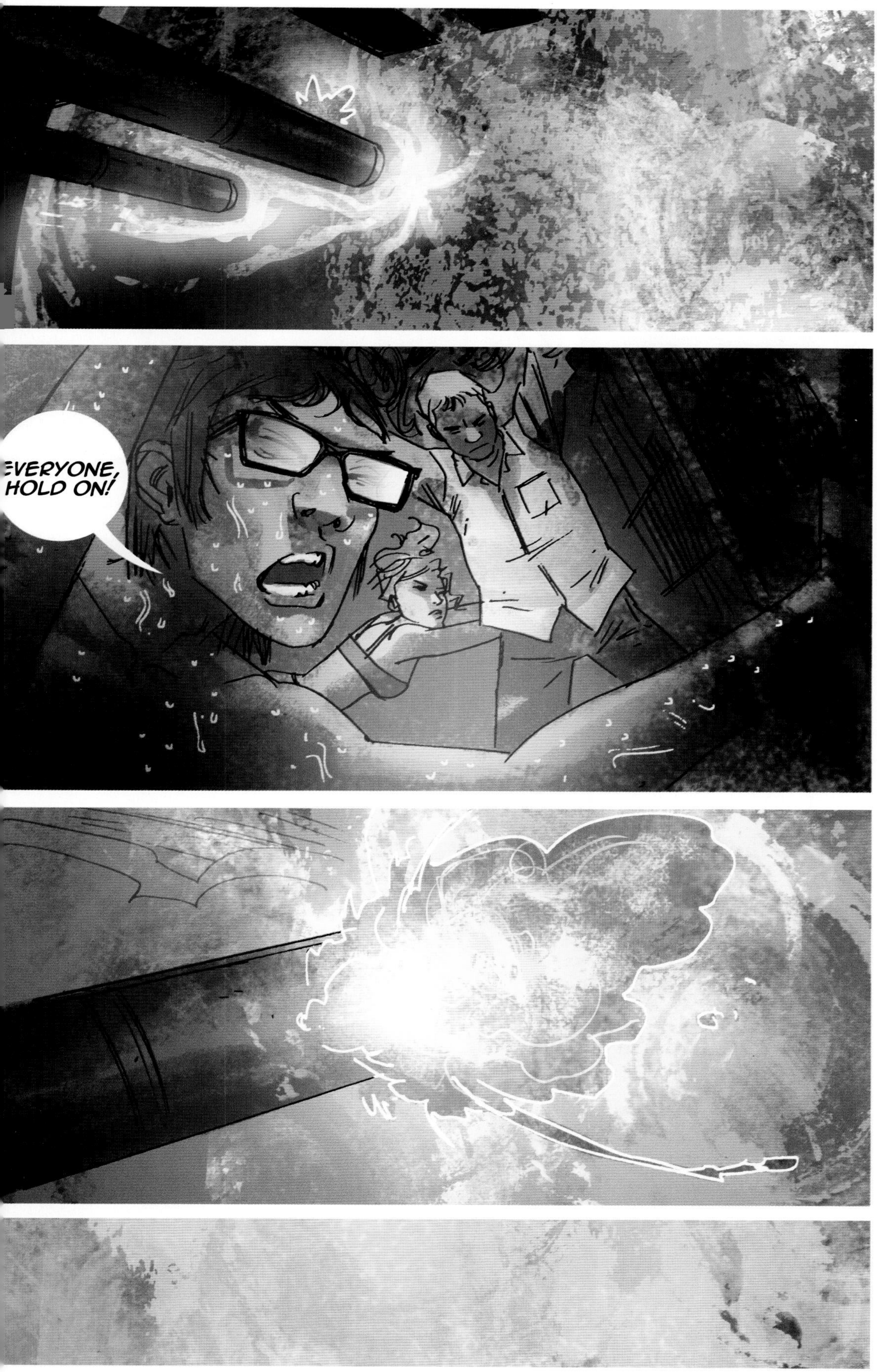
EVERYONE, HOLD ON!

TEMP IS DROPPING.

WE DID IT--

ORBIT IS STABLE, FOR NOW.

HE SAVED US.

YEAH... YEAH, I KNOW.

SO NOW WE START AGAIN. LET'S GET A GROUP OF ENGINEERS TOGETHER TO START TRACKING DOWN ANY OTHER TRAPS THAT MIGHT BE AROUND.

IT'S INCREDIBLY DANGEROUS...I DON'T KNOW IF WE CAN FIND THEM ALL IN TIME--

YEAH, I KIND OF FIGURED THAT.

THAT'S WHY I'M GOING TO GO HAVE A CHAT WITH THE ONE GUY WHO KNOWS WHO DID THIS TO US.

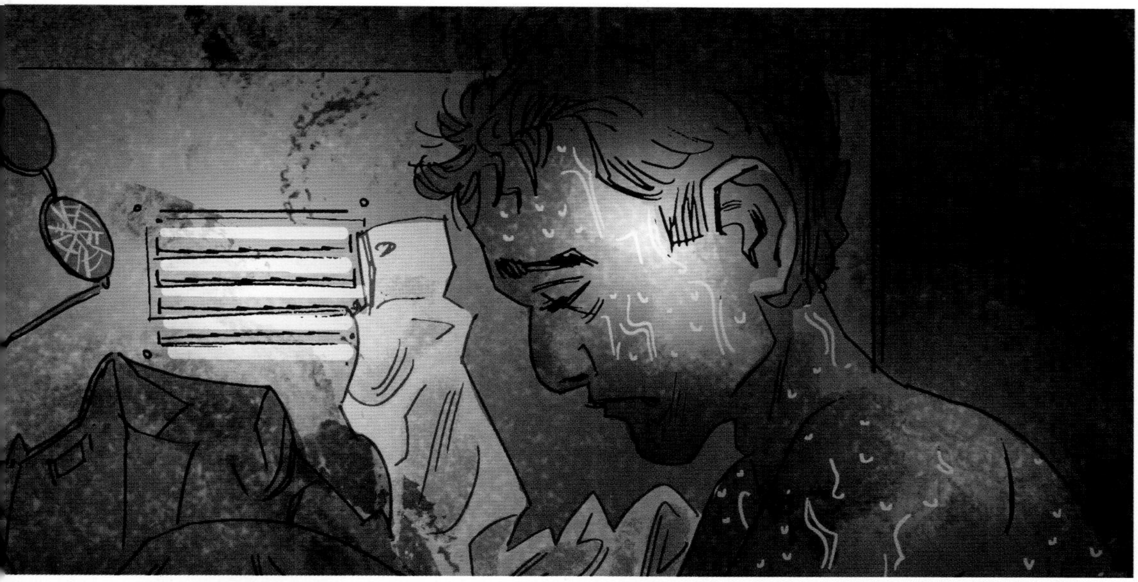

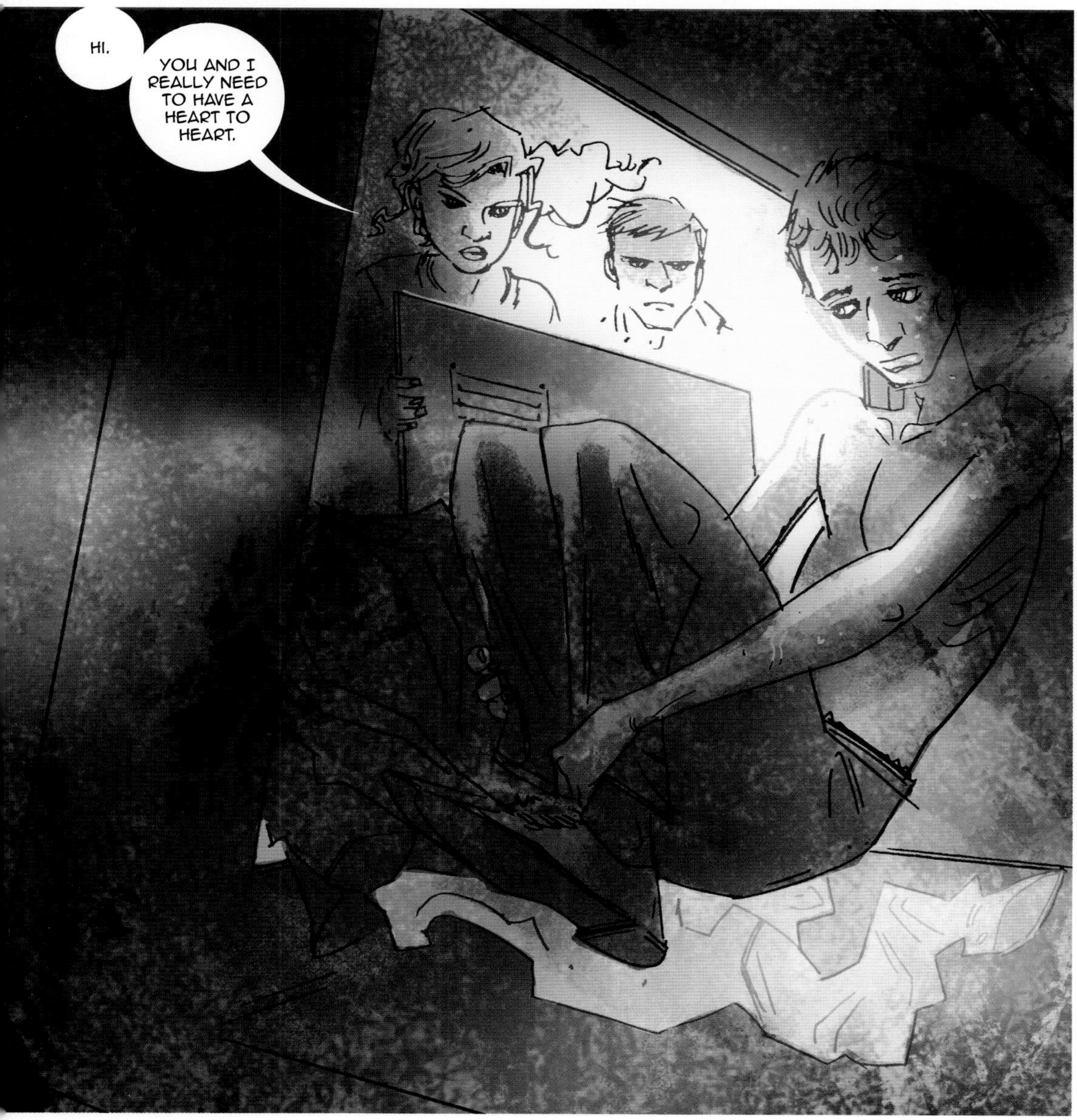
HI.
YOU AND I REALLY NEED TO HAVE A HEART TO HEART.

# CHAPTER TWO

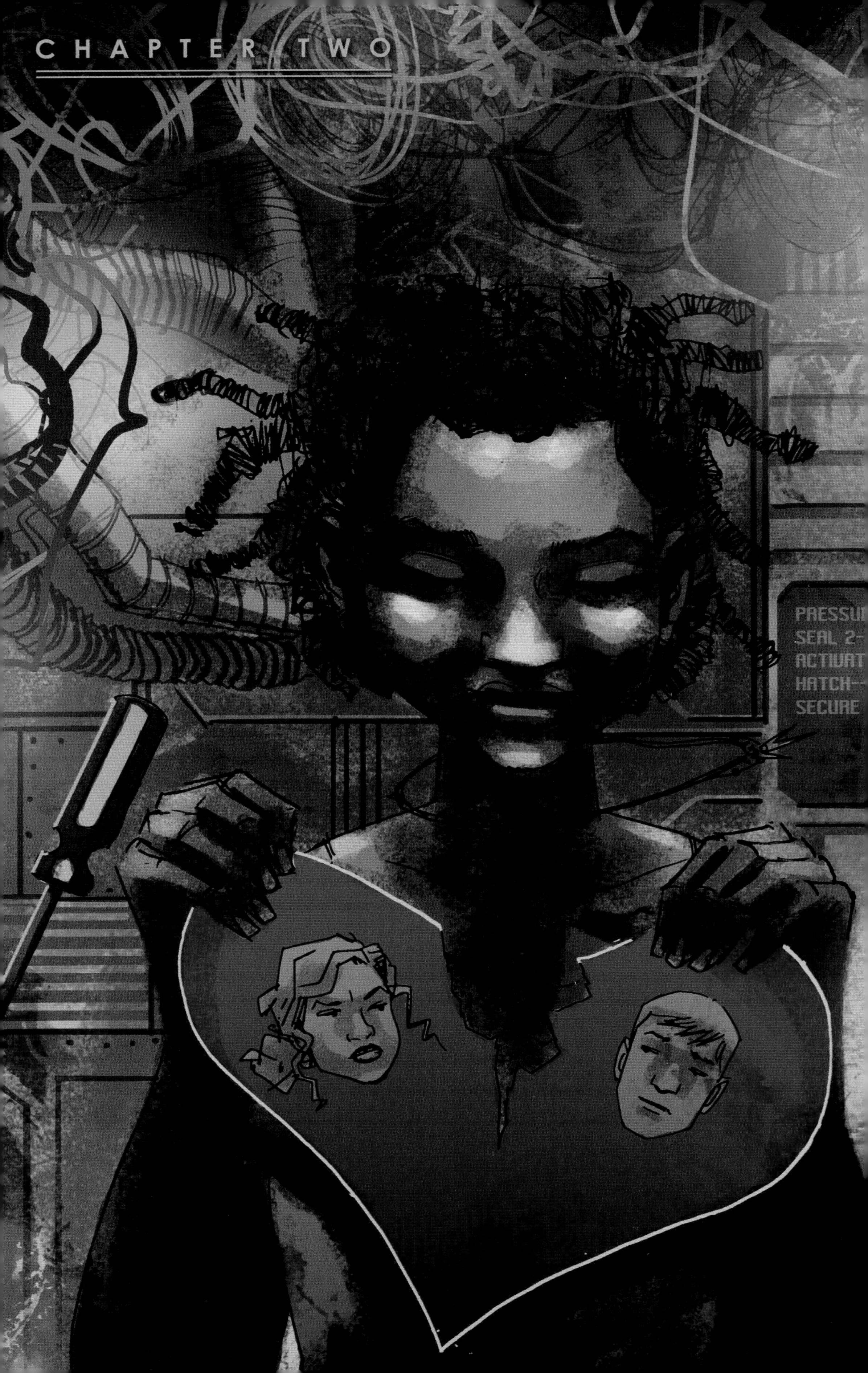
PRESSU
SEAL 2-
ACTIVAT
HATCH--
SECURE

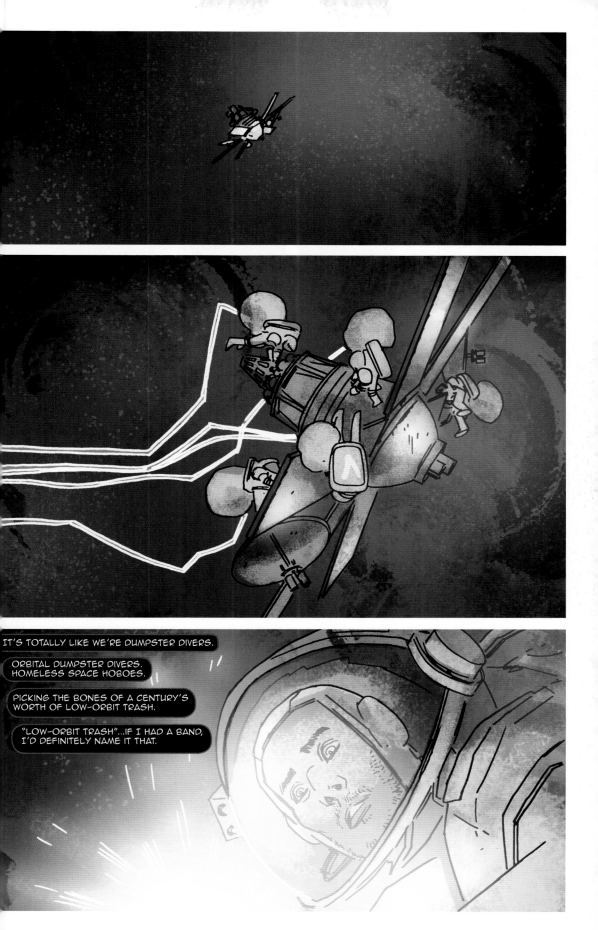

IT'S TOTALLY LIKE WE'RE DUMPSTER DIVERS.

ORBITAL DUMPSTER DIVERS. HOMELESS SPACE HOBOES.

PICKING THE BONES OF A CENTURY'S WORTH OF LOW-ORBIT TRASH.

"LOW-ORBIT TRASH"...IF I HAD A BAND, I'D DEFINITELY NAME IT THAT.

THIS IS OUR FOURTH TIME WE'VE DONE THIS.

WE'VE BEEN UP HERE 45 DAYS. IT'S BEEN 43 SINCE OUR ONLY DEATH.

AND IT'S GOING PRETTY WELL...I GUESS. WE HAVEN'T FOUND ANY MORE BOOBY TRAPS IN THE STATION. EARTH HAS MOSTLY LEFT US ALONE.

BUT THE MORE WE PULL STUFF LIKE THIS... THE MORE I FEEL LIKE THEY'RE GOING TO SIT UP AND TAKE NOTICE.

VERY OUTDATED STUFF IN HERE. MOSTLY OLD CELLULAR-RELAY EQUIPMENT.

BUT LET'S TAKE IT ALL.

I HEARD OTHER VITROS SAYING ALL THE TIME, "I'VE ALMOST FORGOTTEN ABOUT EARTH!"

MYSELF, I FIND IT A LITTLE HARD TO IGNORE.

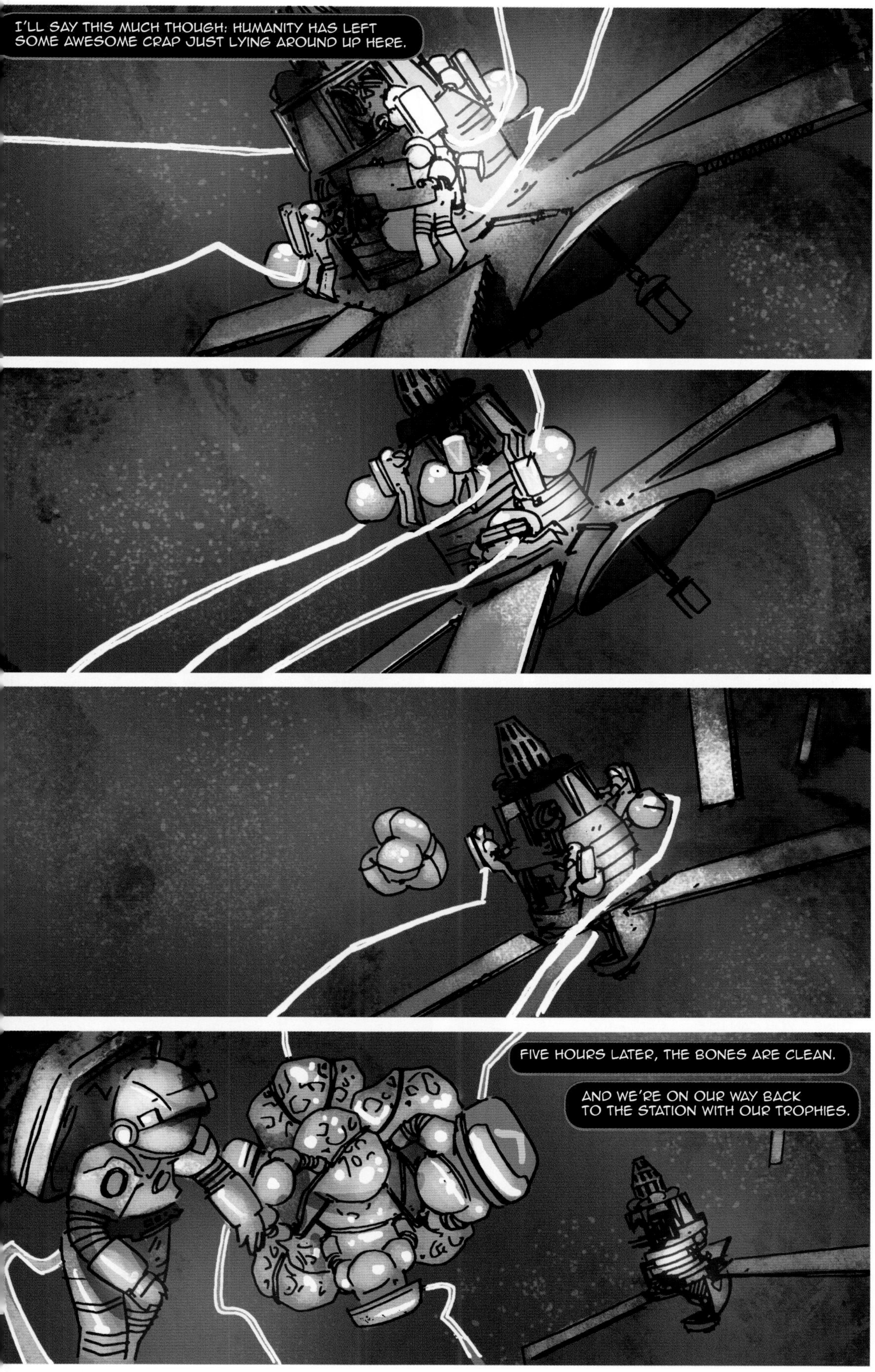
I'LL SAY THIS MUCH THOUGH: HUMANITY HAS LEFT SOME AWESOME CRAP JUST LYING AROUND UP HERE.
FIVE HOURS LATER, THE BONES ARE CLEAN.
AND WE'RE ON OUR WAY BACK TO THE STATION WITH OUR TROPHIES.

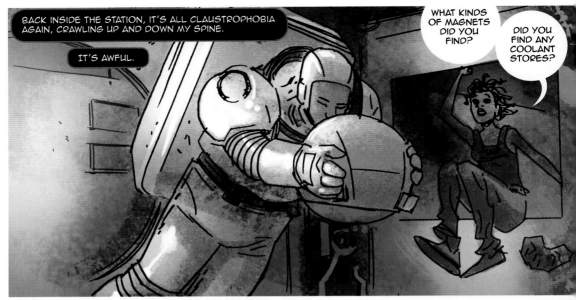

BACK INSIDE THE STATION, IT'S ALL CLAUSTROPHOBIA AGAIN, CRAWLING UP AND DOWN MY SPINE.

IT'S AWFUL.

WHAT KINDS OF MAGNETS DID YOU FIND?

DID YOU FIND ANY COOLANT STORES?

SHE'S GREAT, SAM IS. BUT SHE'S ALSO... A HANDFUL.

I DO NOT KNOW IF YOU'RE UNDERSTANDING *HOW* BADLY I NEED THESE COOLANTS--

YES! I UNDERSTAND.

I CAN'T JUST MAKE THIS STUFF APPEAR. ALL I CAN DO IS BRING BACK WHAT'S OUT THERE.

SORRY, SORRY. LOOK. EVERYTHING WE'VE GOT IS OVER THERE. I THINK WE'VE GOT SOME THINGS YOU CAN USE TO INCREASE THE UTILITY OF THE SUPERCONDUCTOR.

MAGNETS, YES, AND FIELD GENERATORS, MAYBE. COOLANTS? I DOUBT.

SAMANTHA HAS BECOME LIKE OUR LEAD SCIENCE... PERSON...

I ALMOST THINK OF HER LIKE A SCIENCE OFFICER. LIKE THIS IS *STAR TREK* OR SOMETHING.

THE LIST OF MATERIALS SHE NEEDS IS EXTENSIVE AND COMPLICATED AND EVER GROWING. AND WE HA[VE] AN EXTREME SCARCITY OF MATERIALS, FOR OBVIOU[S] REASONS.

THE OTHER THING ABOUT SAMANTHA IS THAT I'M STARTING TO GET A CRUSH ON HER.

BADLY.

NO COOLANTS BUT LOOK AT THIS! PURE SILVER. WE CAN MAKE GREAT USE OF THIS.

AND LOOK AT THIS ADORABLY ANTIQUATED POWER CELL!

IT'S SO CUTE.

PROBABLY USELESS. BUT CUTE.

I DON'T EVEN UNDERSTAND HOW IT HAPPENED. OR WHEN IT HAPPENED.

I MEAN, I HAVE A GIRLFRIEND. AND MY GIRLFRIEND IS GREAT. LILA IS GREAT, REALLY.

I'M SORRY I PESTERED YOU BEFORE. THIS IS A GREAT HAUL. YOU SHOULD COME SEE ME SOON.

I WANT TO SHOW YOU THE PROGRESS WE'VE BEEN MAKING.

FOOD SYNTHESIZING IS UNDERWAY BUT THERE HAVE BEEN SOME OTHER, EVEN MORE EXCITING, DEVELOPMENTS.

LIKE WHAT?

IF I TELL YOU, THERE'S NO REASON FOR YOU TO COME SEE ME, RIGHT?

OH WELL, THERE'D ALWAYS BE A REASON TO COME SEE YOU, SAM.

LILA IS GREAT. I SHOULD BE THINKING ABOUT LILA.

BUT I HARDLY SEE LILA ANYMORE.

SHE'S OBSESSED WITH EARTH.

I'VE TRIED TO GET TO THE HEART OF WHY.

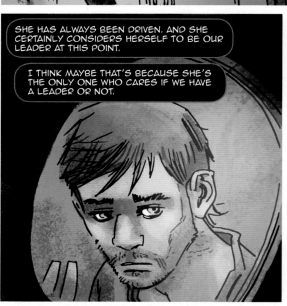

SHE HAS ALWAYS BEEN DRIVEN. AND SHE CERTAINLY CONSIDERS HERSELF TO BE OUR LEADER AT THIS POINT.

I THINK MAYBE THAT'S BECAUSE SHE'S THE ONLY ONE WHO CARES IF WE HAVE A LEADER OR NOT.

WELL, MAYBE NOT THE *ONLY* ONE OF US.

THEY ARE THICK AS THIEVES RIGHT NOW, THOSE TWO.

EVER SINCE SHE WENT DOWN TO CONFRONT HIM.

NOW THEY ARE WORKING TOGETHER. ON A PLAN TO, AND I QUOTE, "DEAL WITH EARTH."

*THEIR* PLAN TO *DEAL* WITH EARTH.

A PLAN SHE WON'T SHARE.

NOT EVEN WITH ME.

SO ARE YOU TWO STILL TOGETHER OR WHAT?

I DON'T KNOW. I'M SURE SHE THINKS WE ARE.

I'M NOT SO SURE I AGREE.

WHY? YOU WANT TO MAKE A PLAY FOR HER?

NOT MY TYPE, I'M AFRAID.

MARKS IS, I THINK, STILL HOLDING A TORCH FOR SOMEONE BACK ON EARTH.

BUT I NEVER ASK HIM ABOUT IT. I FIGURE HE'LL BRING IT UP IF HE WANTS TO.

HELLO. WHAT'S THIS, THEN?

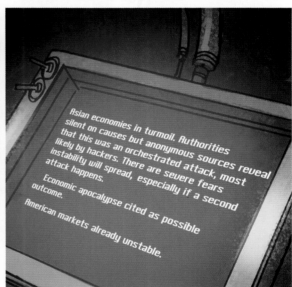

Asian economies in turmoil. Authorities silent on causes but anonymous sources reveal that this was an orchestrated attack, most likely by hackers. There are severe fears instability will spread, especially if a second attack happens.

Economic apocalypse cited as possible outcome.

American markets already unstable.

SO WHAT?

SO...TWO HOURS AGO I CLOCKED A SUDDEN UPSURGE IN ENCRYPTED DATA FROM SOMEWHERE ON OUR STATION.

I DIDN'T FOLLOW THE ROUTING, BUT IT LOOKED LIKE IT WAS TARGETED FOR TOKYO, SHANGHAI, AND, WELL... YOU GET IT.

YOU THINK ONE OF US DID THIS?

IS *THIS* LILA AND HYDE'S GRAND PLAN?

SCREWING AROUND WITH SOME DIGITAL LEDGER SHEETS?

GOD, NO. OF COURSE NOT. WHAT ARE YOU EVEN TALKING ABOUT?

WELL, YOU WON'T TELL ME WHAT YOU *ARE* WORKING ON SO--

WELL, IT'S BETTER THAN THAT. THAT IS A RIDICULOUS, HALF-COOKED PLOT. ECONOMIC INSTABILITY? THAT'S NOT GOING TO STOP OUR ENEMIES. IT'S GOING TO PISS THEM OFF.

I THOUGHT YOU WANTED A WAR WITH EARTH--

NOT A WAR.

A VICTORY.

HER CONFIDENCE STILL STARTLES ME. I DON'T GET IT.

MARKS... HE'S SURE THE SOURCE IS ONE OF US?

YEAH, HE'S SURE.

THE LOGS AND SENSORS WE DO HAVE SHOW A DIRECTED SPIKE OF DATA BOUNCING OFF OF A FEW SATELLITES AND THEN DOWN TO EARTH AT EXACTLY THE TIME THE ATTACKS OCCURRED.

BUT HE DOESN'T KNOW WHO SENT IT?

NO. OUR COMMUNICATION ARRAY DOESN'T SHOW ANY USAGE DURING THE TIME OF THE ATTACK.

GOD DAMN IT, BRANDON. THIS IS EXACTLY THE KIND OF STUFF YOU SHOULD BE KEEPING AN EYE ON WHILE I'M OFF WORKING WITH HYDE.

"KEEPING AN EYE ON"?! THESE PEOPLE ARE OUR FRIENDS, OUR PEERS, OUR EQUALS...NOT A BUNCH OF CHILDREN TO BE WATCHED--

THEY ARE CHILDREN. AND YOU'RE ACTING JUST LIKE THEM NOW. TAKE SOME RESPONSIBILITY.

I'M NOT ENTIRELY SURE, BUT I DON'T THINK THIS IS A HEALTHY RELATIONSHIP RIGHT NOW.

LOOK--

JUST FIND OUT WHO DID IT. AND MAKE SURE THEY DON'T DO IT AGAIN.

WHY DON'T YOU DO IT YOURSELF?

I HAVE BETTER THINGS TO BE DOING.

AND YOU CLEARLY DON'T.

YEAH. SO THAT HAPPENED.

SO NOW WHAT SHOULD LOOK LIKE A ROOM OF MY FRIENDS...

LOOKS LIKE A ROOM OF SUSPECTS.

THIS IS SAMANTHA'S WORKSPACE. BEFORE I CAN ASK SAM ABOUT THE MATTER AT HAND SHE INSISTS ON SHOWING ME WHAT THEY'VE BEEN WORKING ON.

THEY'RE APPLYING ANGULAR ACCELERATORS TO A SUPERCONDUCTOR AND--WELL, IT'S BASICALLY AN ARTIFICIAL-GRAVITY DEVICE. OR IT WILL BE VERY SOON.

THIS ALL SOUNDS GREAT, SAM. BUT I ACTUALLY NEED TO ASK YOU SOME QUESTIONS.

OF COURSE, BRANDON. ANYTHING.

ONE OF US IS MESSING WITH EARTH. AND I NEED TO KNOW IF YOU HAVE ANY IDEA WHO IT IS--

"MESSING"?

YEAH, YEAH, LIKE THEY'RE USING OUR COMM ARRAY TO HACK INTO FINANCIAL MARKETS AND--

SORRY. YEAH. IT'S BORING.

YAWN

ECONOMICS IS THE PSEUDO-SCIENCE OF THE WEAK MINDED.

NO ONE HERE SHOULD HAVE THE TIME OR INTEREST TO DO SOMETHING SO PETTY--

DO YOU KNOW ANYONE WHO MIGHT? I MEAN, YOU DON'T HAVE ALL OF US WORKING IN HERE.

I'D CHECK THE UNDERDECKS. THAT'S WHERE THE LESS SOCIALLY MINDED OF US TEND TO CONGREGATE.

THERE ARE SOME BOYS DOWN THERE WORKING ON A TELEPRESENCE SYSTEM. AND...WELL, THERE IS A LOT GOING ON DOWN THERE. THAT IS WHERE I WOULD LOOK.

DO YOU HAVE ANY IDEA *WHY* ONE OF US WOULD BE DOING THIS? I MEAN, ANYTHING ELSE THAT CAN HELP ME.

I THINK I'VE ALREADY THOUGHT TOO MUCH ABOUT THIS PROBLEM.

BUT I DO WELCOME ANY CHANCE TO SPEAK TO YOU. NEXT TIME HOPEFULLY IT WILL BE ABOUT SOMETHING MORE INTERESTING.

WHAT'D HE WANT?

HE IS PLAYING DETECTIVE.

THE UNDERDECKS.

I ALMOST NEVER COME DOWN HERE.

BY MY COUNT THERE ARE SOME THIRTY ENCLAVES AND CLIQUES DOWN HERE.

THESE THREE ARE TRYING TO SYNTHESIZE A SILK AS STRONG AS A SPIDER'S. I ASK THEM ABOUT EARTH.

I MISS IT--

YOU SHOULDN'T HAVE BROUGHT IT UP, JERK. SHE'LL CRY.

SHE'S ALWAYS CRYING ABOUT EARTH.

SO THEY'RE NOT HIGH ON THE SUSPECT LIST, THEN.

THESE ARE THE THREE SAMANTHA WAS REFERRING TO. THEIR OPINIONS ON EARTH ARE HARDLY SOPHISTICATED.

IT BLOWS.

IT SUCKS.

IT'S GREAT. IF YOU LOVE ASSHOLES, BECAUSE THAT'S ALL YOU'LL FIND THERE.

I'M NOT SURE WHAT IT MEANS THAT SAMANTHA THINKS THREE NINE-YEAR-OLDS HAVE ENOUGH ANGER IN THEM TO RUIN THE EARTH'S ECONOMY.

BUT I FIND IT UNLIKELY.

AND THEN THERE ARE THESE FOUR.

THEY'RE THE ONES THAT FIGURED OUT HOW TO MAKE MANKIND'S FIRST ORBITAL GRAIN ALCOHOL.

WEIGHTLESS AND DRUNK, MAN! IT'S THE BEST.

TRY IT!

IT'LL MAKE YOU VOMIT. SO YOU DEFINITELY GOTTA BE READY TO CATCH IT. DON'T WANT THAT FLOATING AROUND.

I DECLINE THE OFFER.

I CAN'T TELL IF THEY BEAR ANY ILL WILL TOWARDS EARTH. I THINK THEY'RE TOO DRUNK TO BEAR ANY KIND OF WILL TO ANYONE.

I SPEND THE BETTER PART OF A DAY SPEAKING TO VITROS OF EVERY ILK.

I COME AWAY FEELING LIKE WE ARE NOT A COHERENT WHOLE AT ALL. THAT ANY OF THESE PEOPLE MIGHT BE DOING ANYTHING.

I SUDDENLY UNDERSTAND LILA'S FEELING THAT WE NEED A STRONG LEADER TO UNITE US.

MY MOM ALWAYS TOLD ME LISTS WERE THE BEST THING MANKIND EVER INVENTED.

AS I TRY TO SLEEP, I MAKE ONE.

A MASSIVE ECONOMIC SHUTDOWN ON EARTH. ONE OF US HAS DONE IT.

I HAVE A SPACE STATION FULL OF ANGRY TEENAGERS. ANY ONE OF US WITH MOTIVES.

THE COMM TERMINAL IS NOT MONITORED. WE HAVE NO IDEA WHO USED IT WHEN. I'VE HAD THEM PUT A MONITOR ON IT NOW, THOUGH. IF IT HAPPENS AGAIN--WE'LL CATCH THEM. GOOD ENOUGH--

I HATE THESE BUNKS. I CAN'T TOSS AND TURN LIKE I NEED TO BEFORE I SLEEP. I MISS MY BED ON EARTH. AND MY ROOM.

WHAT I SHOULD DO IS PIN IT ON HYDE.

GOD DAMNED RICH KID...STEALING MY GIRLFRIEND...

MAKING ME WANT SAMANTHA.

I KNOW YOU CAN'T *ACTUALLY* FEEL BONE MASS DWINDLING.

BUT I SWEAR I CAN FEEL MY BODY DIMINISHING.

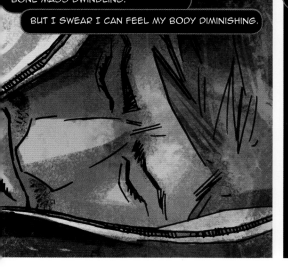

I HAVE A DREAM I'M BACK ON EARTH AND ALL THE REGULAR PEOPLE ARE UP IN SPACE.

BUT BECAUSE THERE AREN'T THAT MANY OF US VITROS, I HAVE A WHOLE CONTINENT TO MYSELF.

AND I AM LONELY.

I NEVER HAVE SEX DREAMS ANYMORE. IT'S AWFUL.

BRANDON. BRANDON, WAKE UP.

WHAT--

IT HAPPENED AGAIN. THE US MARKETS THIS TIME.

WE'RE IN SERIOUS TROUBLE.

WE'VE INTERCEPTED MESSAGES BEING SENT ON EARTH... THEY'RE STARTING TO SUSPECT THAT THE ATTACKS ARE COMING FROM UP HERE. FROM US.

DAMN IT. GET SOME REST. WE'LL THINK BETTER WITH SOME SLEEP.

I ASKED YOU TO DO ONE THING: STOP THIS. AND YOU HAVEN'T DONE IT.

THERE'S WORK TO BE DONE. I'LL SLEEP NEXT WEEK--

A CHARMER, MY GIRLFRIEND.

SO THE WORLD ECONOMY IS HEADED FOR DISASTER BECAUSE OF A FEW DEVIOUS ATTACKS LAUNCHED FROM THIS DEVICE.

AFTER THE FIRST ATTACK I HAD A TRACKER INSTALLED ON THIS THING.

IT TRACKED EXACTLY ZERO BYTES OF OUTGOING DATA LAST NIGHT.

YOU'RE THINKING THAT THERE IS NO EVIDENCE HERE TO HELP YOU.

AND THAT MEANS TWO THINGS.

HELLO, MAUDSLEY.

ONE: THAT THE VITRO DOING THIS HAS MADE HIMSELF, OR HERSELF, A TRANSMITTER THAT YOU DO NOT KNOW ABOUT.

AND TWO: THAT YOU ARE TERRIBLE AT RATIOCINATION.

BUT IT'S OKAY, WE ALL HAVE OUR FAULTS.

ROBERT MAUDSLEY, INFAMOUS ON EARTH, HAS REMAINED STRANGELY UNDER THE RADAR SINCE WE GOT UP HERE.

IS THAT YOUR WAY OF OFFERING TO HELP?

IT'S MY WAY OF SAYING THE ANSWER SHOULD BE OBVIOUS.

AND IF YOU FEEL THE NEED TO ASK FOR MY HELP...I WOULDN'T SAY NO.

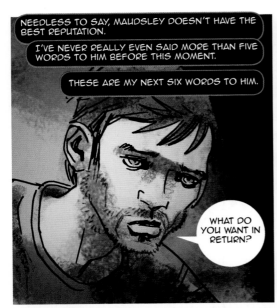

NEEDLESS TO SAY, MAUDSLEY DOESN'T HAVE THE BEST REPUTATION.

I'VE NEVER REALLY EVEN SAID MORE THAN FIVE WORDS TO HIM BEFORE THIS MOMENT.

THESE ARE MY NEXT SIX WORDS TO HIM.

WHAT DO YOU WANT IN RETURN?

I KNOW HE'S BEEN A BIT BUSY, BUT HE HASN'T UPHELD HIS PART OF THAT DEAL.

BACK ON EARTH, HYDE MADE A DEAL WITH ME TO GET ME TO COME QUIETLY.

I WANT YOU TO GET ME IN WITH THEM LILA AND HYDE.

I DON'T KNOW HOW I'M SUPPOSED TO DO THAT.

WE'LL FIGURE SOMETHING OUT. YOU AND ME. TOGETHER.

WE'LL BE FRIENDS. AND WHEN YOU CAN HELP ME... YOU WILL.

CONSIDER THIS LITTLE OFFERING OF HELP AS A TOKEN.

I DIDN'T KNOW HIM ON EARTH.

BUT SUDDENLY...HE SEEMS LIKE A PRETTY GOOD FRIEND TO HAVE.

ALL RIGHT, SO WHO IS BEHIND THE ATTACKS?

ATTACKS? NO ONE. THESE AREN'T ATTACKS.

THIS IS A PRANK. STUPID, JUVENILE, AND POINTLESS. IF SOMEONE WANTS TO SEE AN ATTACK... THEY SHOULD HAVE ASKED ME.

AND BECAUSE IT IS JUST A PRANK, WE HAVE TO LOOK AT THE PSYCHOLOGY OF IT AS SUCH.

I THINK WE'RE LOOKING FOR A RICH KID. A PARTICULARLY SPOILED ONE. THE KIND THAT WOULD TOILET PAPER HIS OWN HOUSE. OR EGG THE BMW DADDY DRIVES AROUND IN.

DON'T LOOK AT THE MACRO. LOOK AT THE MICRO.

AND YOU'LL FIND YOUR CULPRIT.

THERE YOU GO. M. BELKNAP-LONG HAS LOST BILLIONS MORE THAN THE OTHER BILLIONAIRES.

FIND OUT WHICH OF US HAS A PERSONAL CONNECTION TO HIM AND YOU'LL HAVE FOUND YOUR PRANKSTER.

1. M. Belknap-Long
2. Jerry Grant
3. Harvey Props
4. Gladys Roe

YOU KNOW YOU'RE IN BAD SHAPE WHEN SUDDENLY ROBERT MAUDSLEY IS YOUR BEST FRIEND IN THE WHOLE UNIVERSE.

MICHAEL BELKNAP-LONG JR. LIVES IN THIS ROOM.

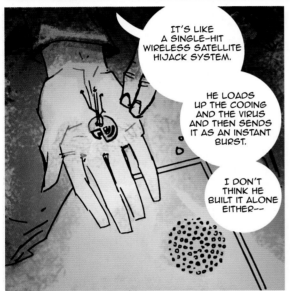

IT'S LIKE A SINGLE-HIT WIRELESS SATELLITE HIJACK SYSTEM.

HE LOADS UP THE CODING AND THE VIRUS AND THEN SENDS IT AS AN INSTANT BURST.

I DON'T THINK HE BUILT IT ALONE EITHER--

Y'KNOW, IF YOU'RE ACTUALLY INTERESTED IN CREATING SOME SENSE OF ORDER AROUND HERE, YOU SHOULD PROBABLY CREATE A BETTER DATABASE OF WHO IS ON BOARD--

AND WHO THEIR PARENTS ARE. OTHERWISE THIS KIND OF PETULANT-CHILD ACTIVITY MIGHT RUN RAMPANT--

HEY! WHAT ARE YOU GUYS DOING IN MY BUNK?!

YOU CAN'T BE IN HERE!

WE KNOW WHAT YOU'VE BEEN DOING, MIKE--

JUST COME QUIETLY--

REALLY? "JUST COME QUIETLY"?

WHAT'S NEXT? "AFTER HIM"?

I HADN'T THOUGHT ABOUT WHAT TO SAY WHEN WE FOUND HIM!

HE WENT THAT WAY.

HEY!

YOU GUYS DON'T UNDERSTAND, OKAY?

THAT MAN WAS NEVER ANYTHING BUT A DICK TO ME AND THEN HE GETS ME SENT UP HERE? I CAN JUST SEE HIM COUNTING HOW MUCH MONEY HE'S GOING TO SAVE NOW HE DOESN'T HAVE TO WORRY ABOUT ME!

JUST COME DOWN AND WE'LL TALK IT OUT, OKAY?

YOU DO REALIZE HE HAS ALL OF THE SHIP CONTROLS UP THERE.

IF HE TOUCHES THE BUTTON, HE COULD LOCK US ALL IN HERE AND DEPRESSURIZE THIS WHOLE SECTION OF THE SHIP.

YEAH, I'M AWARE.

I HAVE A SOLUTION, THOUGH.

YEAH?

WHEN SHE PRESSES THE BUTTON I SUDDENLY FEEL SOMETHING I HAVEN'T FELT IN MONTHS.

HEY! WHAT ARE YOU DOING?

HAVE YOU EVER THOUGHT ABOUT HOW TO DESCRIBE HOW GRAVITY FEELS? NEITHER HAVE I.

BUT THAT'S WHAT I FEEL.

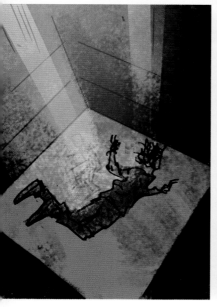

THE ARTIFICIAL GRAVITY IS WORKING.

WELCOME TO THE FLOOR.

SO MARKS USED MIKE'S SINGLE-BLAST BOX TO PIN THE WHOLE THING ON A RIVAL TRADER.

AND MIKE HAS JOINED UP WITH THE BURGEONING TELEPRESENCE PROGRAMS.

AS FOR LILA AND ME...

LOOK, WE NEED TO TALK, LILA.

YEAH, TONIGHT. LATER.

SHE STILL WON'T TELL ME WHAT THE HELL THEIR BIG SECRET IS.

COME IN, LILA.

COME IN, LILA.

THIS IS HAL ROBERTS. LAST VITRO ON EARTH, READY TO RECEIVE ORDERS.

# CHAPTER THREE

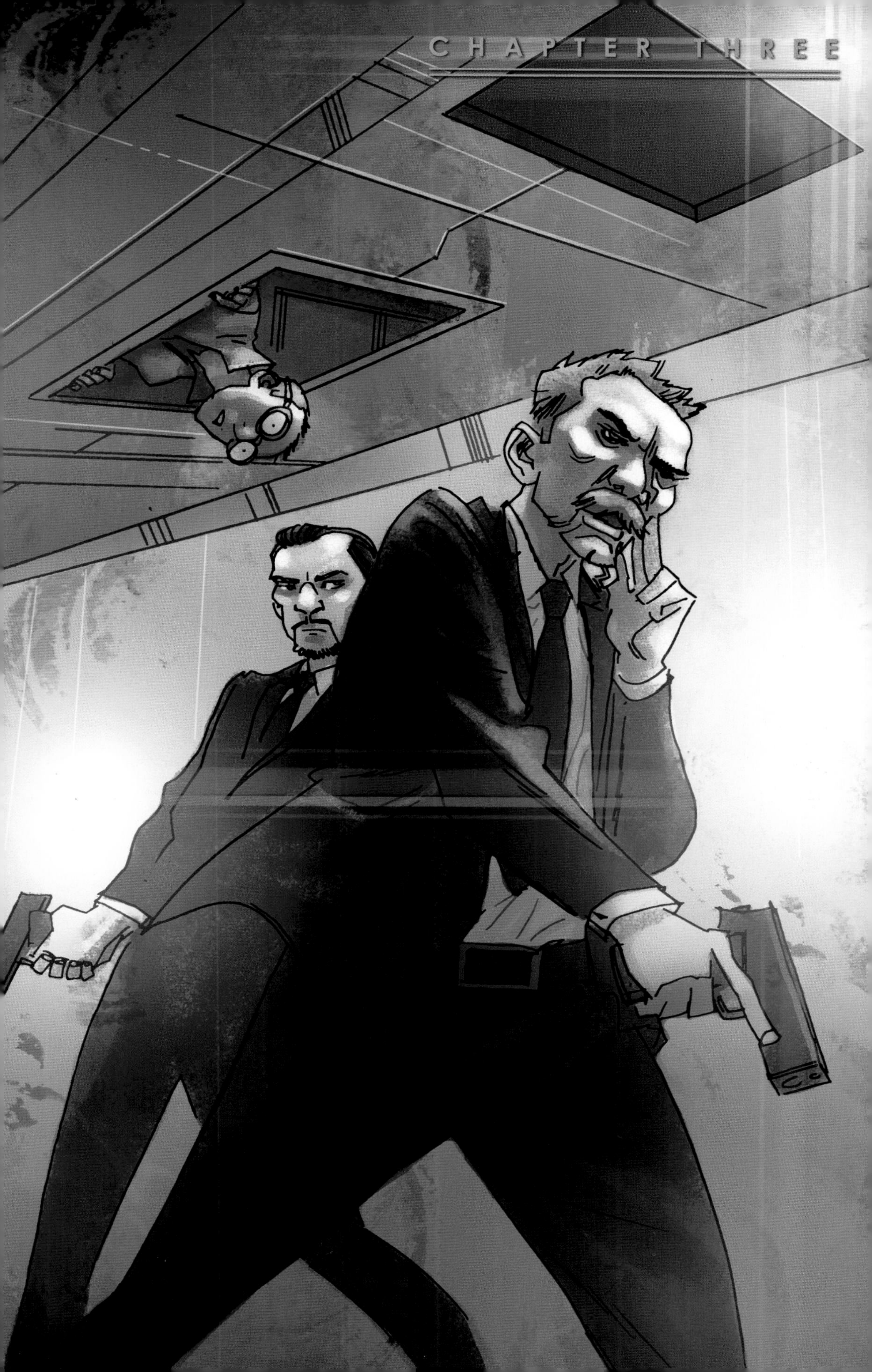

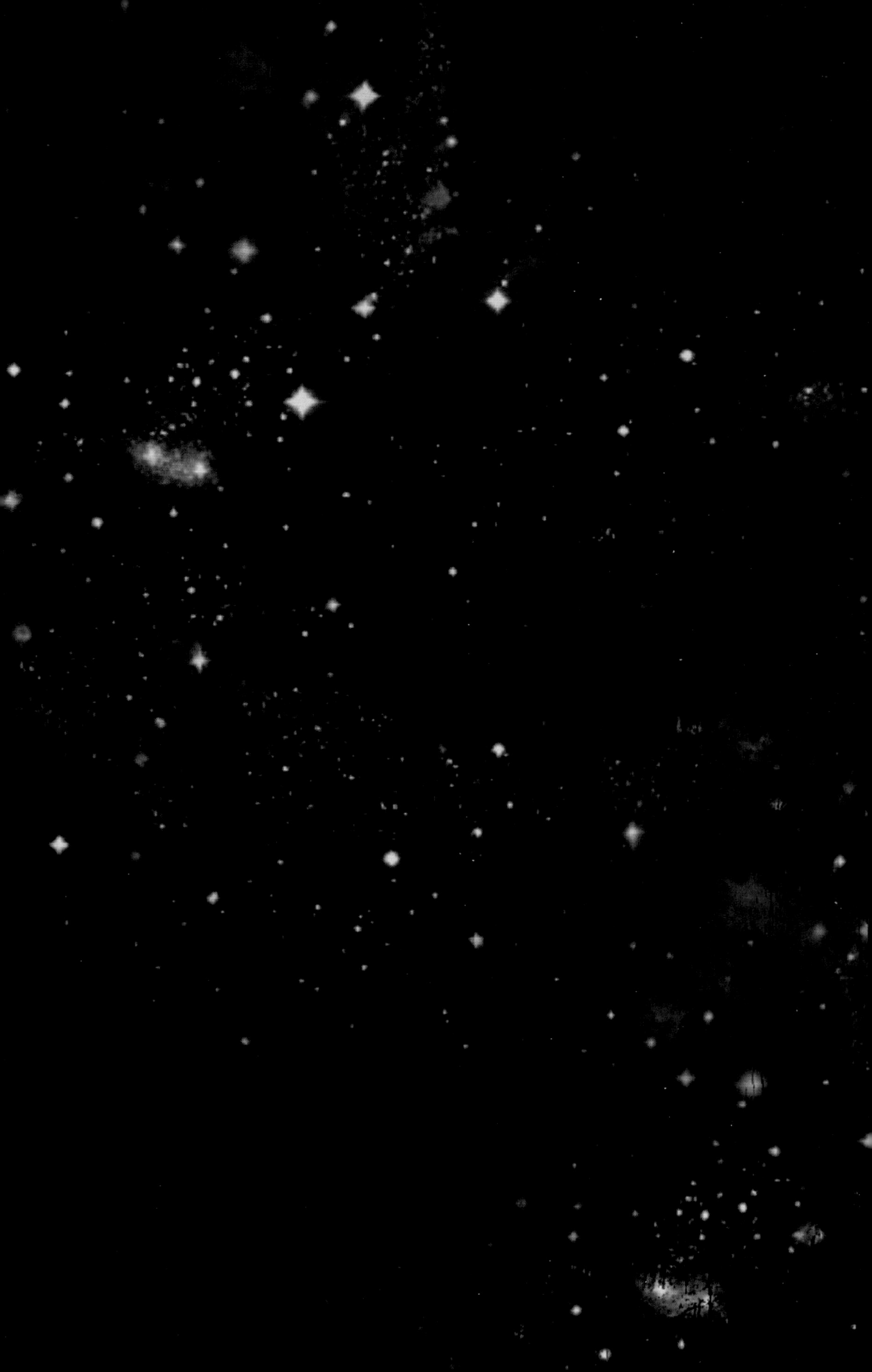

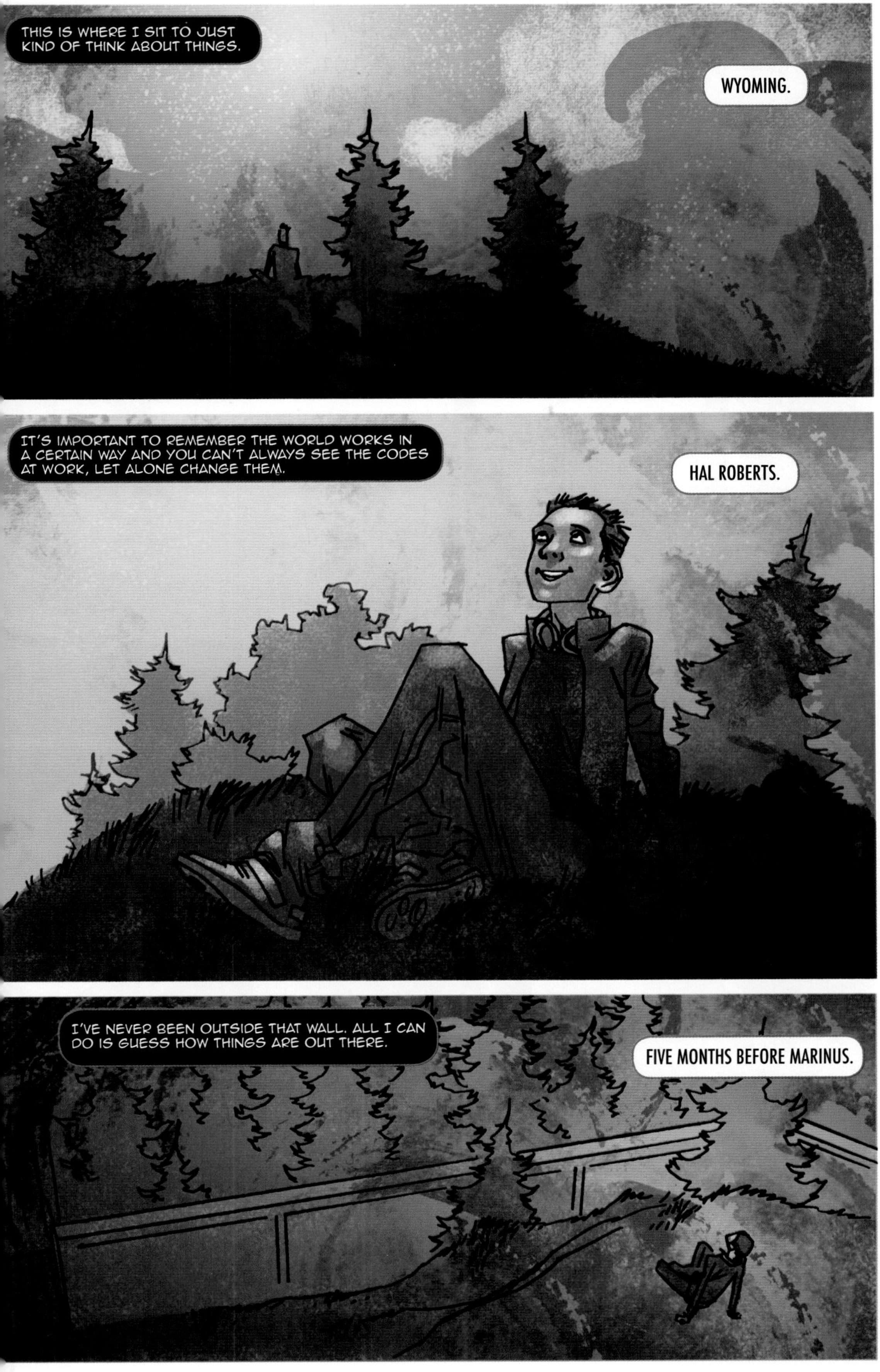
THIS IS WHERE I SIT TO JUST KIND OF THINK ABOUT THINGS.
WYOMING.
IT'S IMPORTANT TO REMEMBER THE WORLD WORKS IN A CERTAIN WAY AND YOU CAN'T ALWAYS SEE THE CODES AT WORK, LET ALONE CHANGE THEM.
HAL ROBERTS.
I'VE NEVER BEEN OUTSIDE THAT WALL. ALL I CAN DO IS GUESS HOW THINGS ARE OUT THERE.
FIVE MONTHS BEFORE MARINUS.

THIS IS MY HOUSE.

IT IS WHAT IT LOOKS LIKE IT IS: A BIG OL' COMPOUND. MEANT TO SURVIVE ANY APOCALYPSE YOU CAN NAME AND A FEW I BET YOU'VE NEVER EVEN CONSIDERED.

IT WAS BUILT BY MY PARENTS, WHO... WELL--

--THEY HAVE CERTAIN *ISSUES* WITH THE IDEA OF A FEDERAL GOVERNMENT. CALL THEM RUGGED INDIVIDUALISTS.

AND THAT'S HOW THE FOUNDING FATHERS FOUGHT OFF THE OPPRESSIVE KING GEORGE.

AND THAT'S HOW A WELL-TRAINED, WELL-ARMED MILITIA DEFEATED THE US ARMY.

I DON'T THINK THERE'S ANY OTHER WAY TO FIGURE IT, SON.

PARANOIA IS A SURVIVAL INSTINCT.

TO LET IT GO IS TO INVITE *THEM* IN.

KNOW WHAT YOU'RE THINKING: "A FAMILY OF NUTJOBS."

BUT THEY DON'T HAVE ANY OF THE SUPER CRAZY IN THEM. LIKE, FOR EXAMPLE, THEY BELIEVE IN SCIENCE; HELL, THEY MADE ME WITH SCIENCE. THEY'RE NOT TRYING TO MAKE THE WORLD ADHERE TO ANY ARCHAIC RELIGIOUS STANDARDS.

THEY'RE JUST TRYING TO LIVE A LITTLE MORE FREE.

AND THE THING IS, THEY WERE RIGHT TO BE PARANOID.

THEY WERE TOTALLY RIGHT.

COME ONE MORE STEP TOWARDS MY SON AND I START SHOOTING.

IF HE DOESN'T COME WITH US NOW, OTHERS WILL COME FOR HIM.

LEAVE.

THEY DON'T.

I HADN'T BEEN PLANNING FOR THIS, SPECIFICALLY.

BUT I DID HAVE AN EMERGENCY PACK PREPARED. AND WHEN THE MOMENT CAME, I WAS ALREADY GONE.

PARANOIA IS A SURVIVAL MECHANISM, AFTER ALL.

LIVE FREE

TARGET IS LOOSE.

I LOVED MY PARENTS, YEAH, DEFINITELY.

BUT I HAD ALWAYS PLANNED ON BREAKING FREE AT SOME POINT. AND I HAD FANTASIZED ABOUT THIS MOMENT: THE FIRST BREATH OF AIR BEYOND THE WALL.

IT ISN'T LIKE I IMAGINED. IT'S SCARIER AND MORE EXCITING.

THE SHADOWS SEEM SOMEHOW DIFFERENT. MORE FREE AND THEREFORE MORE DANGEROUS.

I'VE NEVER MET ANOTHER VITRO. I DON'T KNOW HOW SMART THEY ARE, WHAT THEY KNOW. ANY OF THAT.

I'M *GOOD* WITH SYSTEMS AND LANGUAGES AND CODES.

LIKE...REAL GOOD. LIKE SOMETIMES I DON'T EVEN THINK IN ENGLISH.

MY THOUGHTS COME IN SOME *OTHER* LANGUAGE, MORE TECHNICAL...I DON'T EVEN KNOW WHAT YOU'D CALL IT. SOMETHING NEW.

>>>LARAMIE COUNTY SHERIFFS DEPARTMENT.

Accessing JOHN DOE BODIES...

+JOHN DOE. 47 year old, white male, found with stab wound.

+JOHN DOE. 14 year old, white male, found starved to death.

+HAL ROBERTS. 14 year old, white male found starved to death.

I GAMBLED A BIT SEEING THEM ONE LAST TIME.

BUT I HAD TO SEE THEM ONE LAST TIME.

FOR EMOTIONAL REASONS, SURE. BUT ALSO BECAUSE I NEEDED THEM TO KNOW THAT THEY HAD TO LIE. AND THAT I WOULD BE OKAY.

IF YOU GUYS COULD JUST COME THIS WAY.

WE DO NEED YOU TO IDENTIFY THE BODY.

FRANKLIN HYDE COMES OUT AS VITRO

I WAS PRETTY MOVED BY WHAT HYDE SAID. I MEAN, I'D NEVER MET HIM BEFORE BUT THAT SEEMED PRETTY COOL. PRETTY ON THE MONEY.

STAND UP. PROCLAIM WHAT YOU ARE, IN A LOUD VOICE. SCREW 'EM IF THEY CAN'T HANDLE IT.

LITTLE-KNOWN FACT ABOUT THE GAMEFOG ONLINE SERVICE: THEIR SECURITY PROTOCOLS ARE TOP NOTCH.

THEY'VE WON FOUR COURT CASES PREVENTING THE FBI, THE CIA, AND THE NSA FROM ACCESSING THEIR USER INFORMATION AND COMMUNICATIONS.

GAMEFOG

HYDE- MY NAME'S HAL. YOU DON'T KNOW ME BUT I'M ONE OF YOU. I'M NOT COMING WITH YOU WHEREVER YOU'RE GOING BUT I DIG IT WHAT YOU'RE TRYING TO DO. GET IN TOUCH WITH ME HERE IF YOU EVER NEED TO.

LOOK AT THIS KID. MAKES ME SICK. YOU CAN TELL HE THNKS HE'S BETTER THAN US.

I DON'T SEE WHY THEY DON'T JUST TURN THEMSELVES IN. IF THEY'RE SO INNOCENT, WHAT DO THEY HAVE TO HIDE?

Tickets

I HAD THIS SUDDEN FEELING, NO IDEA WHERE IT CAME FROM, REALLY, THAT I NEEDED TO TAKE STEPS TO KEEP THE REALITY OF MY SITUATION VERY WELL HIDDEN.

SO, AS A FUGITIVE TEEN, HOW DO YOU LIVE A HIDDEN LIFE?

I MADE MYSELF AN ALIAS, A FULL-ON ALTERNATE VERSION OF MYSELF: "HALBROOK JOHNSON, WEB ADMINISTRATOR."

AND THEN I FUNDED HIM UP, SET UP AN ONLINE BANK ACCOUNT, GOT HIM AN APARTMENT, CREDIT CARDS, DELIVERY GROCERY SERVICE...

...VIDEO GAMES. HALBROOK JOHNSON *LOVES* VIDEO GAMES.

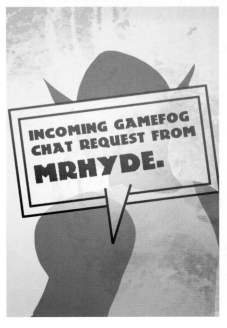

INCOMING GAMEFOG CHAT REQUEST FROM **MRHYDE.**

I GOT, LIKE, ALL NERVOUS.

I MEAN...IT WAS KIND OF LIKE THE PRESIDENT WAS CALLING. I MEAN SURE, I'D SLIPPED HIM MY NUMBER.

BUT STILL...

IS IT WORKING?

HE'S RIGHT THERE!

HI.

UH.

HOW'S IT GOING?

WE'RE TRAPPED IN SPACE, SO IT'S NOT GOING VERY WELL.

HOW DO WE KNOW THIS COMMUNICATION IS SECURE?

I RATTLE OFF THE SECURITY PROTOCOLS I HAVE IN PLACE ON TOP OF THE GAMEFOG LOCAL SYSTEMS.

AND I NOTE THAT THE GOVERNMENT DOESN'T NEED TO TRACK THEIR SIGNAL; IT ALREADY KNOWS WHERE THEY ARE.

IF THE CONNECTION ISN'T SECURE, I'M THE ONE IN DANGER.

I'M SATISFIED WITH ALL THAT.

HOW DO WE KNOW YOU ARE WHAT YOU SAY YOU ARE?

BECAUSE OF THIS.

ONE OF THE OTHER LITTLE THINGS I'VE BEEN WORKING ON.

HEY!

YOU DID THAT?

YEP.

I WAS BORED LAST WEEK, SPENT SOME TIME CUTTING MY WAY INTO THE OLD NASA SERVERS AND THEN JUMPING FROM THEM TO THESE NEW RUSSIAN SOLYDAT NUMBERS THEY HAVE FLOATING UP THERE.

AND USING THEIR SERVERS, I WAS ABLE TO SEND A PING INTO YOUR LIGHTING CIRCUITS.

I'M SATISFIED WITH THAT.

HAL, YOU ARE ABOUT TO BECOME THE KEY PLAYER IN VITRO FREEDOM.

AWESOME.

THEIR FIRST QUESTION: "HOW DO YOU FEEL ABOUT INFILTRATING A GOVERNMENT BUILDING?"

JUST FINE, I SAID. I FEEL JUST FINE ABOUT THAT.

PAPA WOULD BE SO PROUD.

ABOUT A WEEK LATER, I'M NECK DEEP N SURVEILLANCE.

THIS IS THE NSSTA.

NATIONAL SPACE SECURITY TRANSITIONAL AUTHORITY.

THE BASTARDS IN CHARGE OF "TENDING" THE VITRO SATELLITE. THEY HANDLE THE SATELLITE'S ORBIT CORRECTION, LIFE SUPPORT. THEY RUN THE SURVEILLANCE AND TRACKING. THEY'RE LIKE HIGH-STAKES PRISON WARDENS.

ACCORDING TO HYDE, THE NSSTA WAS STARTED ABOUT TWENTY YEARS AGO TO "TRANSITION" THE NATION INTO AN ERA OF CHINESE SPACE SUPERIORITY.

THE POLITICAL WILL TO GET THAT DONE EVAPORATED.

BUT THE PROPER POLITICAL WILL TO SCREW THE VITROS?

NEVER A SHORTAGE OF THAT.

SO, SECURITY IS, LIKE, WAY TIGHT.

LIKE, THIS WON'T BE EASY AT ALL.

DID YOU THINK IT WOULD BE?

WELL, IT'S DIFFERENT ACTUALLY *SEEING* IT, NOT JUST THINKING ABOUT HOW IT WOULD BE.

ANYWAY. HERE'S WHAT WE GOT.

I RUN DOWN THE FULL LIST FOR THEM. NEVER LESS THAN SIX MANNED GUARD POSTS. BASELINE CAMERA SURVEILLANCE BACKED UP BY A MORE HEAVY-DUTY CAMERA CLOUD SURVEILLANCE SYSTEM.

THE BUILDING HAS A THOUSAND EYES. THAT'S WHAT THIS MEANS.

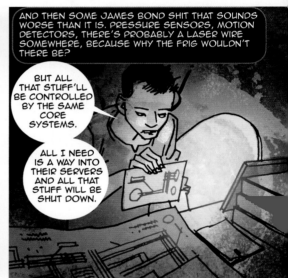

AND THEN SOME JAMES BOND SHIT THAT SOUNDS WORSE THAN IT IS. PRESSURE SENSORS, MOTION DETECTORS, THERE'S PROBABLY A LASER WIRE SOMEWHERE, BECAUSE WHY THE FRIG WOULDN'T THERE BE?

BUT ALL THAT STUFF'LL BE CONTROLLED BY THE SAME CORE SYSTEMS.

ALL I NEED IS A WAY INTO THEIR SERVERS AND ALL THAT STUFF WILL BE SHUT DOWN.

IN THE NEGATIVE CATEGORY, THOSE SERVERS WILL BE HIDDEN DEEP INSIDE THE BUILDING AND THE TRIGGERS I'LL NEED TO DISARM THEM WILL BE HIDDEN INSIDE THE LARGER CODE IMPRINT OF THE ENTIRE PLACE.

SO, NOT *QUITE* SO SIMPLE.

I THINK THAT'S IT..?

A WEEK LATER, I'M DROWNING IN A SEA OF CODE.

I'VE WRITTEN PROGRAMS AND VIRUSES AND WHATEVER BEFORE, OBVIOUSLY. BUT THIS ISN'T THAT. NOT AT ALL.

THIS IS WAR. AND I'M CREATING A CODE ARMY.

MEANWHILE, MY COCONSPIRATORS WERE WORKING ON WAYS TO GET PAST ALL THAT SECURITY STUFF.

I NEVER SAW A SINGLE OTHER VITRO WORKING ON ANYTHING. I'M NOT SURE IF THEY BROUGHT ANYONE ELSE IN ON THE PLANS OR NOT.

EVERYTHING THEY DESIGNED, THEY'D SEND DOWN TO A LITTLE 3-D PRINTER I SET UP IN THE CORNER.

I WISH I COULD HAVE TOLD MY PARENTS WHAT I WAS UP TO.

THEY'D HAVE LOVED IT.

THE DAY GETS CLOSE AND I GET A BIT NERVOUS.

7:02 PM.

HI THERE! I'M SAM'S KID, UP ON FOUR?

employee directory

I HIT HIM WITH A PHEROMONE ENHANCER. IT MAKES THE SPEAKER SEEM HONEST, INNOCENT. COMPLETELY TRUSTWORTHY.

MY CLOTHES'RE LACED WITH A KIND OF VISUAL GAUSSER. PUMPS OUT MAGNETIC FIELDS OF VARYING DEGREES OF INTENSITY.

ENOUGH TO CONFUSE THE FIRST-TIER SURVEILLANCE EQUIPMENT.

UPPER-LEVEL SECURITY'S A BIT MORE TRICKY. MORE GUARDS, MORE CAMERAS, MORE LOCKS.

POISON, BUT NOT A CHEMICAL COMPOUND. SYNTHETIC. CODE THAT WRITES ITSELF INTO THE SPINE.

IT WON'T KILL THEM, BUT THEY'LL BE OUT FOR HOURS.

THIS IS WHERE THE KNOT STARTS TO TIGHTEN.

IF I CAN'T LOCATE THE RIGHT TERMINAL I CAN'T SWITCH OFF THE THIRD-TIER SECURITY.

AND THEIR MAP PROGRAM IS CRAP. TERMINALS AREN'T LABELED WITH, OR LOCATED BY, ANY DISCERNIBLE PATTERN.

WITH TEN MINUTES TO SPARE, I DECIDE TO WING IT.

"WING IT" IN THIS CASE MEANS TURN MY HANDHELD DEVICE INTO AN ELECTROMAGNETIC IMPRINT LOCATOR.

AND THEN FIND THE SERVERS ON FOOT.

BUT THAT MEANS I NEED MOBILITY.

I'M TRAPPED ABOVE THESE TWO CLOWNS.

FOR FIVE MINUTES THEY BARELY MOVE.

YAWN

I'M LOOKING FOR A CERTAIN DENSITY OF PULSE AND CHARGE IN THE AIR.

THAT'LL LEAD ME TO THE SERVER HUB.

I'M CLOSE.

FOR A MINUTE, I FEEL LIKE I CAN SMELL THE CODE IN THE AIR AROUND ME.

BEEP

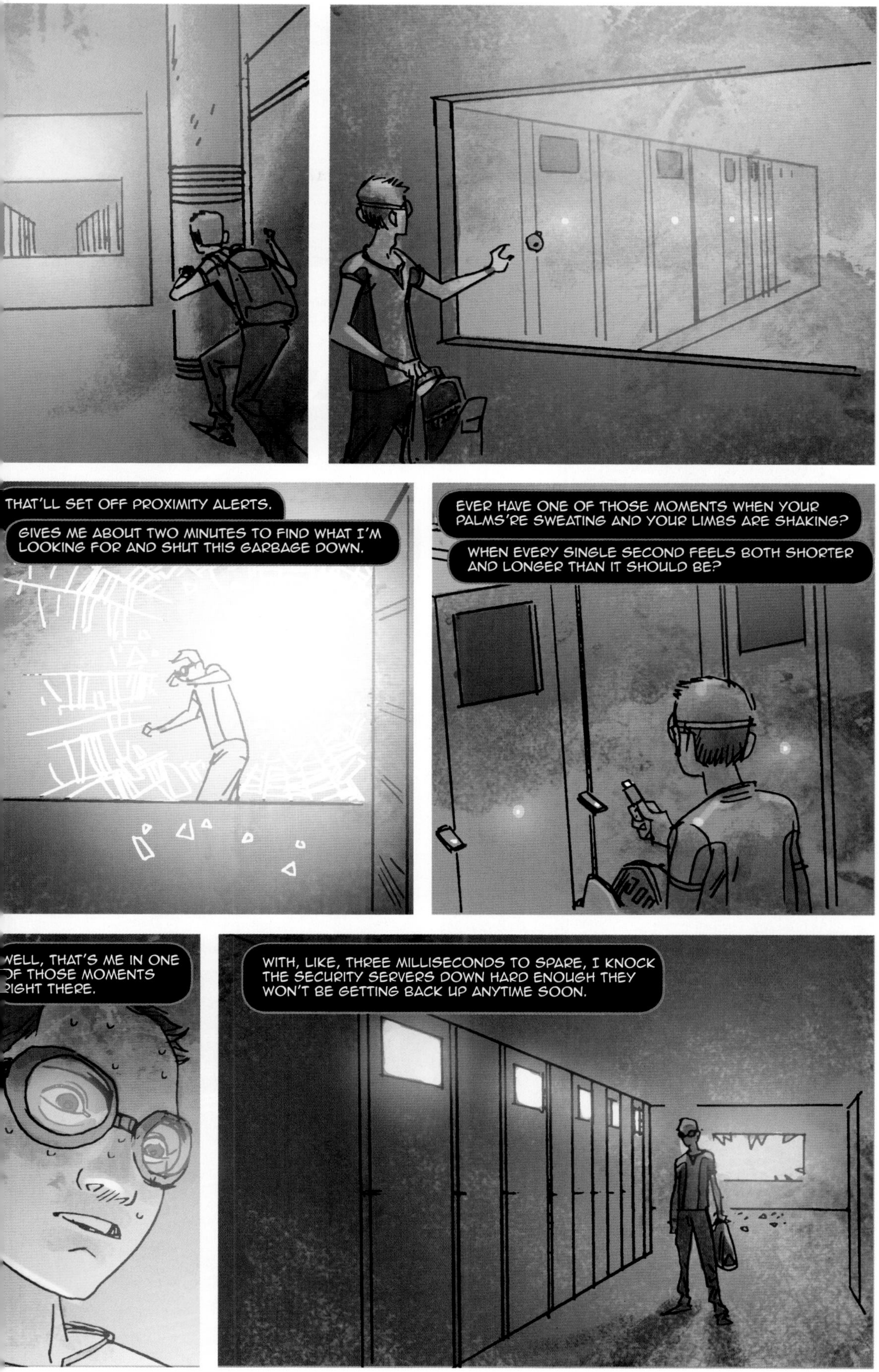
THAT'LL SET OFF PROXIMITY ALERTS.
GIVES ME ABOUT TWO MINUTES TO FIND WHAT I'M LOOKING FOR AND SHUT THIS GARBAGE DOWN.
EVER HAVE ONE OF THOSE MOMENTS WHEN YOUR PALMS'RE SWEATING AND YOUR LIMBS ARE SHAKING?
WHEN EVERY SINGLE SECOND FEELS BOTH SHORTER AND LONGER THAN IT SHOULD BE?
WELL, THAT'S ME IN ONE OF THOSE MOMENTS RIGHT THERE.
WITH, LIKE, THREE MILLISECONDS TO SPARE, I KNOCK THE SECURITY SERVERS DOWN HARD ENOUGH THEY WON'T BE GETTING BACK UP ANYTIME SOON.

AND THEN I STROLL ON IN TO THE CONTROL ROOM, TRYING TO LOOK COOL EVEN THOUGH MY HANDS ARE STILL WAY CLAMMY.

ANY PROBLEMS?

NAH. NOT REALLY.

MY ARMY OF CODE MARCHES INTO THE SATELLITE SYSTEMS. IT SETS UP CAMP.

1263DRT7770A377
ENTRY CODE ALPHA 46L01
...DIRECTORY LOGIN SUCCESS!
5LOG-276VALUE3
X IS EQUAL TO ALPHA VALUE
X-5684533-55-2657778

AND IT BEGINS TO WAGE WAR.

STARTING THE UPLOAD NOW.

THE PLAN: TRANSFER ALL SERVER DATA ON THE VITROS UP TO THE SATELLITE.

THEN ERASE IT ALL WITH SUCH THOROUGHNESS THAT IT WILL NEVER BE RETRIEVED.

KNOCK THE SATELLITE SYNC OUT OF WHACK, PERMANENTLY.

BY THE TIME THE SUN RISES, THE VITRO WILL BE LOST TO THE WORLD. TOTALLY FREE.

RUN PROGRAM? ■

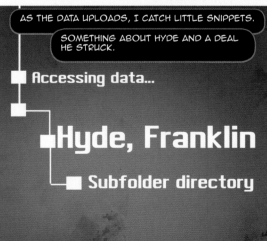

AS THE DATA UPLOADS, I CATCH LITTLE SNIPPETS.

SOMETHING ABOUT HYDE AND A DEAL HE STRUCK.

■ Accessing data...

■ Hyde, Franklin

■ Subfolder directory

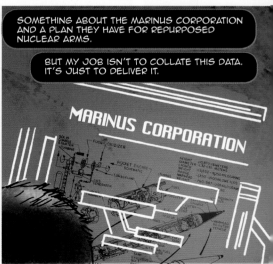

SOMETHING ABOUT THE MARINUS CORPORATION AND A PLAN THEY HAVE FOR REPURPOSED NUCLEAR ARMS.

BUT MY JOB ISN'T TO COLLATE THIS DATA. IT'S JUST TO DELIVER IT.

MARINUS CORPORATION

THE GAMEFOG SYSTEM IS SECURE BUT IT'S NOT *THAT* SECURE. THEY'LL BREAK IT EVENTUALLY. SO THE FINAL PART OF THE PLAN IS ENDING ALL COMMUNICATION BETWEEN ME AND THEM.

ONCE THIS IS DONE, I WILL BE TRULY ALL ALONE.

HEY HAL, I KNOW WE WON'T SEE EACH OTHER ANYMORE AFTER THIS. BUT I JUST WANTED TO SAY THANKS.

HEY, DON'T MENTION IT.

EMOTION WAS NEVER MY STRONG SUIT.

YOU GUYS READY TO DISAPPEAR COMPLETELY?

WITHOUT A SINGLE DOUBT.

GOODBYE.

SIGNAL LOST

I SPEND AN HOUR DOUBLE CHECKING THE WORK, REENFORCING THE CODE. I GET A LITTLE LOST IN IT, TO BE HONEST.

ESCAPE WAS ALWAYS SUPPOSED TO BE THE EASIEST PAR

MAYBE THAT'S WHY I LOST TRACK OF TIME. OVERCONFIDENCE OR SOMETHING.

OR MAYBE I WAS JUST HAVING TROUBLE LETTING THE MOMENT BE OVER.

HEY!

STILL, I'M NOT REALLY IN TROUBLE WHEN THE GUARDS SEE ME.

I'M NOT EVEN REALLY IN TROUBLE WHEN THE BACKUP SECURITY SYSTEM REBOOTS.

AND I HAVE ENOUGH ANTIPERSONNEL ORDNANCE ON ME TO DROP THESE GUYS.

I'M IN A BIT OF TROUBLE WHEN I FIND A LOCKED DOOR THAT WAS SUPPOSED TO BE UNLOCKED.

FIVE ARMED GUARDS. AND I HAVE NOWHERE TO RUN.

THAT'S WHEN I'M IN DEEP TROUBLE.

BUT STILL, JOB'S DONE.

AND I CAN'T STOP SMILING.

BECAUSE I KNOW THEY'LL ASK ME TO UNDO THE CODE.

AND I KNOW I COULDN'T EVEN IF I WANTED TO.

IT'S NOT MY CODE ANYMORE; IT'S ITS OWN CODE. IT'S SELF-REPLICATING, SELF-MUTATING, SELF-IMPROVING.

SO WHERE AM I, ANYWAY? SOME KIND OF GOVERNMENT BLACK SITE OR SOMETHING?

YOU'RE MOSTLY RIGHT. BUT THIS ISN'T A GOVERNMENT-RUN BLACK SITE.

IT'S A BLACK SITE RUN BY THE MARINUS CORPORATION.

WE'VE TAKEN OVER VITRO ADMINISTRATIVE DUTIES. YOU PROVED THE GOVERNMENT'S INADEQUACY WITH YOUR LITTLE STUNT.

SO WE'VE STEPPED IN.

I DIDN'T SEE THIS COMING.

WE'RE GOING TO DO WHAT THE GOVERNMENT COULD NOT.

WE'RE GOING TO EXTERMINATE THE VITROS.

THE WORDS HANG IN THE AIR A MOMENT. I FIND MYSELF UNABLE TO SAY A WORD IN RETORT.

I JUST WANTED YOU TO KNOW. THE MISSILES LAUNCH AT DAWN.

VERY SOON YOU WON'T JUST BE THE LAST VITRO ON EARTH. YOU'LL BE THE LAST VITRO. PERIOD.

WE'LL TALK AGAIN SOON.

I KNOW THE CODE WAS GOOD ENOUGH THAT THEY'D NEVER HAVE LOCK CAPABILITIES.

IT'D BE DIFFICULT...ALMOST IMPOSSIBLE TO HIT THE SATELLITE.

*ALMOST* IMPOSSIBLE.

IF THEY MANAGED TO FIND THE SATELLITE AGAIN THROUGH SOME OTHER MEANS, THEY COULD BASICALLY USE OLD MORTAR-LOBBING TECHNIQUES TO HIT IT. FIRE A MISSILE, SEE IF IT HITS, CORRECT TRAJECTORY, TRY AGAIN.

WORLD WAR I-ERA WAR TECHNIQUES TRANS-POSED INTO THE NUCLEAR SPACE AGE.

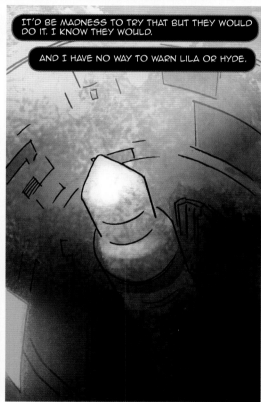

IT'D BE MADNESS TO TRY THAT BUT THEY WOULD DO IT. I KNOW THEY WOULD.

AND I HAVE NO WAY TO WARN LILA OR HYDE.

HOPE I CAN FIGURE A WAY OUT IN TIME.

PROPULSION SYSTEM IS LIVE.

PREPARE FOR FIRST LAUNCH.

# CHAPTER FOUR

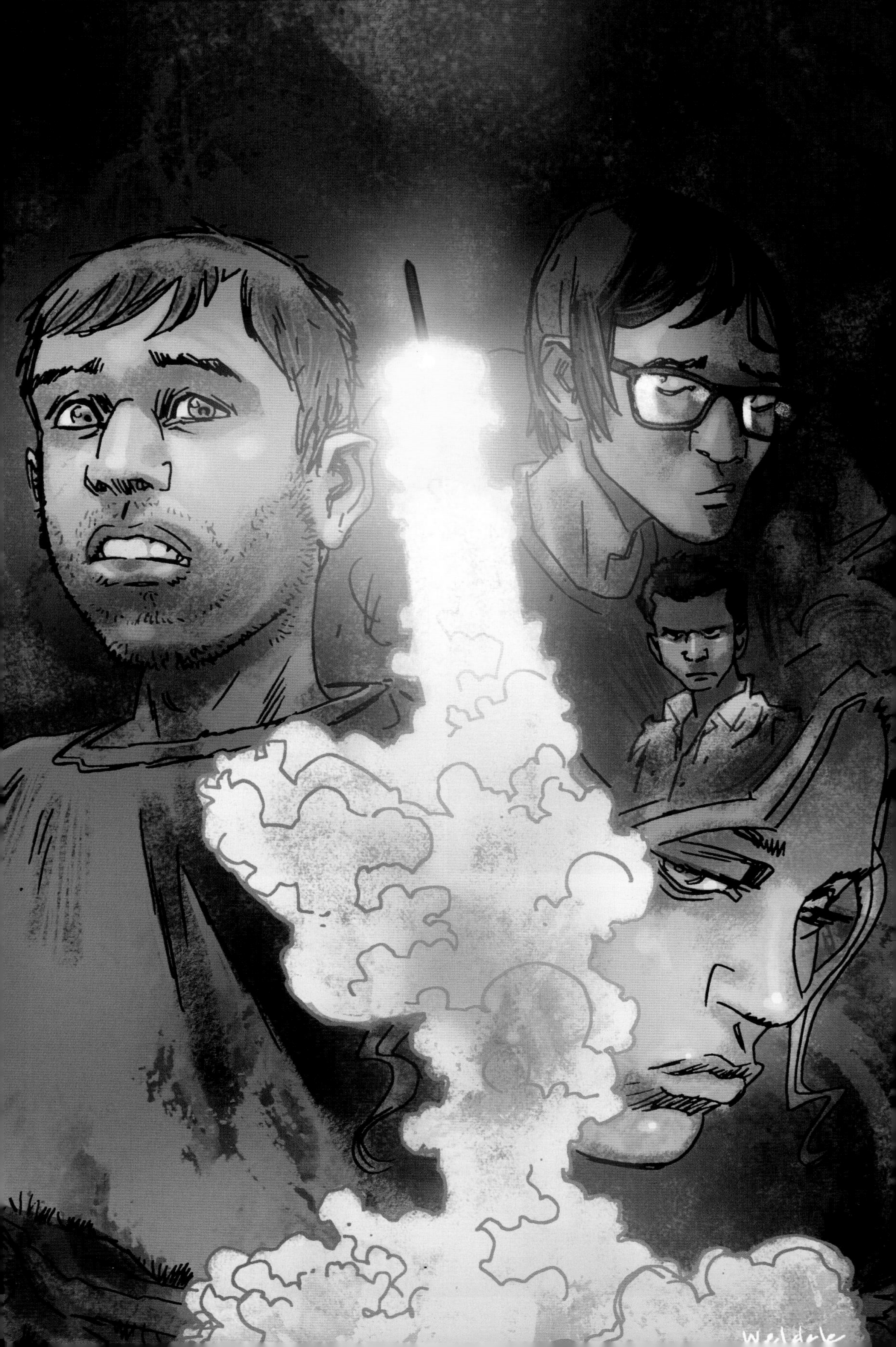

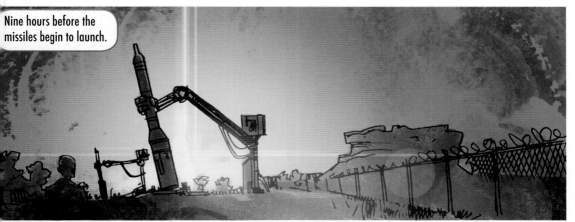

Nine hours before the missiles begin to launch.

Meanwhile, on the station.

LET'S ADJUST THE METADENSITY TO A LEVEL WHERE THE WELL IS OBSERVABLE BY THE HUMAN EYE.

COOL.

CLICK!

READY?

READY.

THERE WE GO--

YEAH. WAY COOL.

HEY, YOU GUYS GOTTA CLEAR OUTTA HERE. SAM'S GOING TO USE THIS SPACE TO SET UP A MEDICAL LAB--

BUT--

OUT!

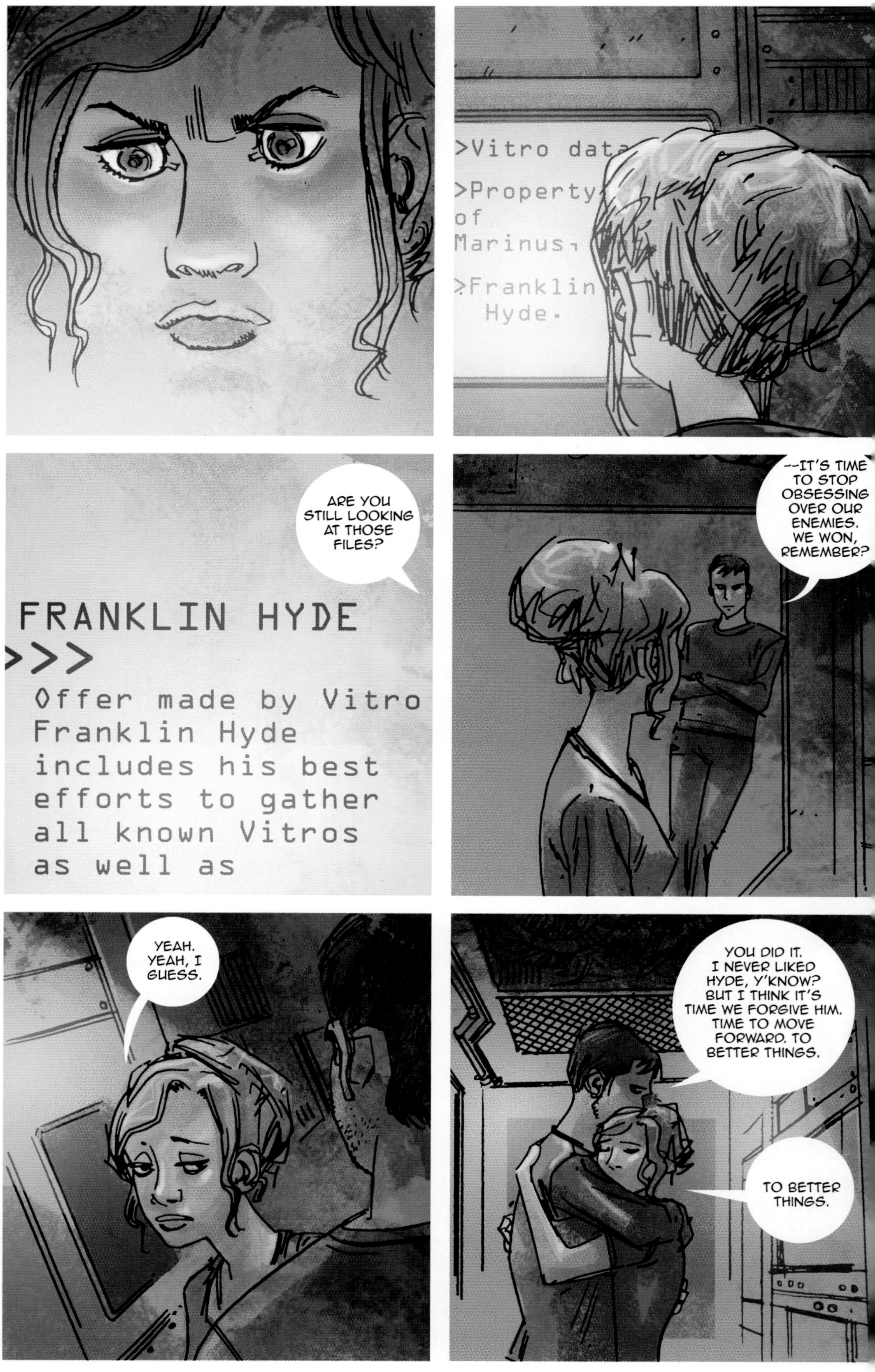

>Vitro data
>Property of Marinus,
>Franklin Hyde.
ARE YOU STILL LOOKING AT THOSE FILES?
FRANKLIN HYDE
>>>
Offer made by Vitro Franklin Hyde includes his best efforts to gather all known Vitros as well as
--IT'S TIME TO STOP OBSESSING OVER OUR ENEMIES. WE WON, REMEMBER?
YEAH. YEAH, I GUESS.
YOU DID IT. I NEVER LIKED HYDE, Y'KNOW? BUT I THINK IT'S TIME WE FORGIVE HIM. TIME TO MOVE FORWARD. TO BETTER THINGS.
TO BETTER THINGS.

TODAY WE ARE FREE FROM EARTH.

OUR FUTURE IS OUR OWN TO STEER--

WHAT THE HELL IS THE TRAITOR DOING UP THERE WITH YOU!?

YEAH! I THOUGHT WE WEREN'T EVER GOING TO HAVE TO SEE HIS FACE AGAIN!

HE'S NOT A TRAITOR. IT WAS HIS PLAN THAT FREED US. WE HAVE TO *TRY* TO PUT WHAT HE DID BEHIND US.

DO YOU MIND IF I SAY A FEW WORDS?

UH--

I DON'T THINK THAT'S A GOOD--

A NEW ERA IS UPON US...

BUT LET'S NOT FORGET WE'VE ALL SUFFERED TO GET HERE. AND ALL BECAUSE OF WHAT?

BECAUSE OF HOW WE WERE BORN: AN ACCIDENT OF SCIENCE AND FATE.

I NEVER INTENDED FOR US TO BE UP HERE--NEVER INTENDED FOR US TO HAVE BEEN PUT THROUGH SO MUCH.

BUT WE WERE, BECAUSE MEN ON EARTH BETRAYED US. BETRAYED ME.

THAT BETRAYAL IS OVER. WE ARE FREE. WE CAN DO AS WE WANT.

TODAY WE ARE FREE TO MAKE THE FUTURE WE WANT!

THIS REMINDS ME OF THAT TIME WE WERE ALL DRUGGED AND BLASTED INTO SPACE.

YEAH, THAT WAS A GOOD TIME, WASN'T IT?

HAVING THOSE TWO THINKING THEY'RE OUR LEADERS-- IT CAN'T END WELL.

WELL, WHO ELSE IS GOING TO DO IT? YOU?

MAYBE I'M WRONG. MAYBE EVERYTHING WILL BE FINE.

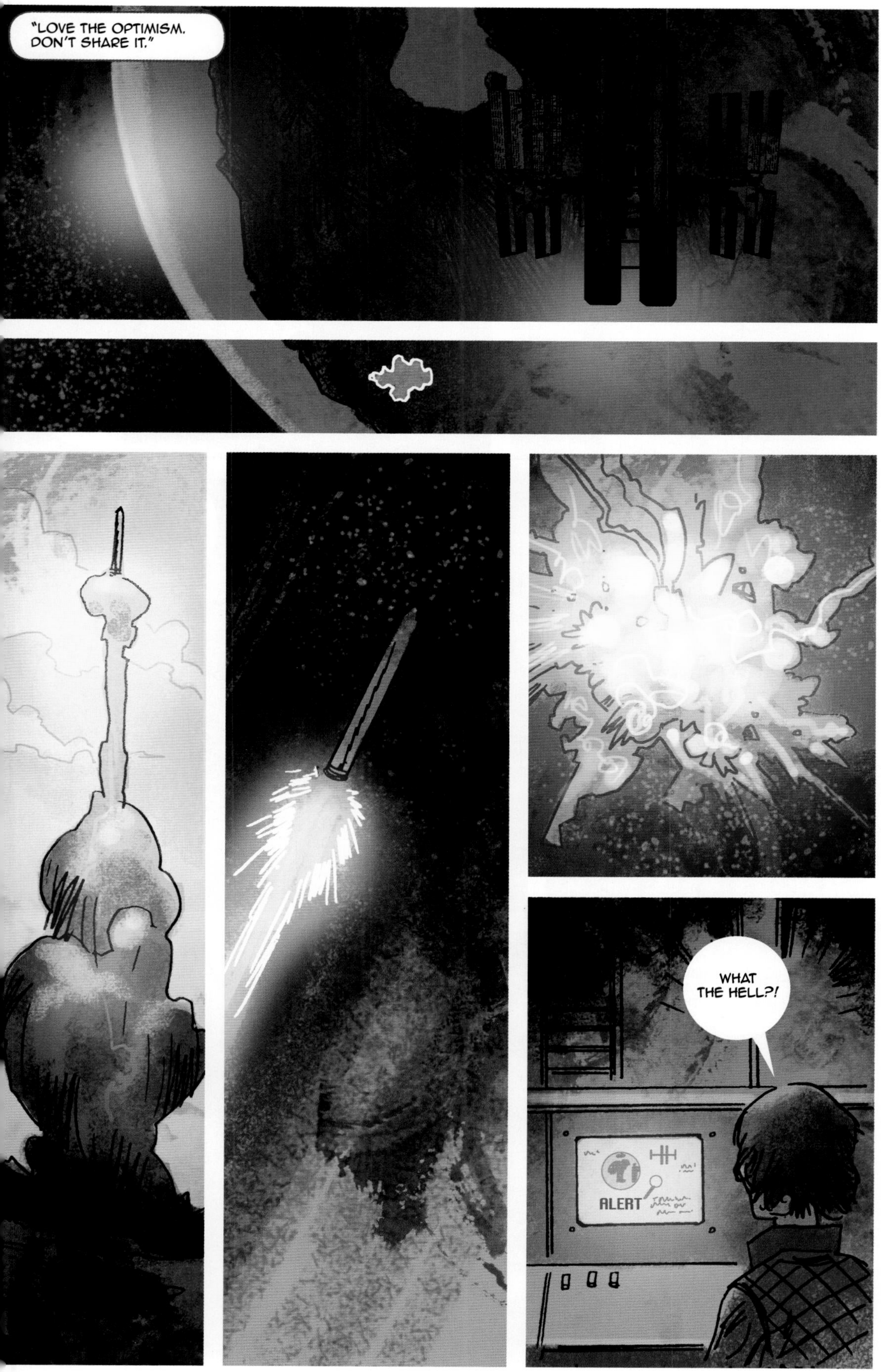
"LOVE THE OPTIMISM. DON'T SHARE IT."
WHAT THE HELL?!
ALERT

NUKES. ARE YOU KIDDING ME?!

WISH I WAS.

WHAT GOVERNMENT WOULD BE CRAZY ENOUGH--

IT'S NOT A GOVERNMENT.

IT'S MARINUS. THEY BOUGHT HUGE STOCKS OF NUKES IN A CONTRACT TO DESTROY THEM.

WELL, THEY CLEARLY TOOK A LOOSE DEFINITION OF "DESTROY."

FIRST MISSILE DETONATED OVER AFRICA.

SECOND SOMEWHERE OVER ASIA. THEY'RE MILE OFF OF US--

THEY DON'T HAVE TARGETING DATA. SO WHAT THE HELL ARE THEY DOING?

ARE THEY JUST GOING TO TOSS MISSILES INTO ORBIT, HOPING THEY'LL HIT US?

THEY'RE BEING SMART.

"IT'S TRUE THEY DON'T HAVE ANY KIND OF SYNC ON OUR POSITION.

"THESE MISSILES, THIS LAUNCH PATTERN, IT'S MEANT TO TRIANGULATE ON OUR POSITION.

"THEY CAN'T SEE *US* ON THEIR TARGETING COMPUTERS. BUT THEY CAN SEE THE ATMOSPHERIC EFFECTS OF THEIR OWN EXPLOSIONS."

EACH MISSILE THEY DETONATE WILL BRING THEM CLOSER TO OUR POSITION.

5,312 miles from station

AND WHEN THEY FIND US-- WELL...

THAT'S INSANE!

THAT'S WHAT THEY DO.

THAT'S WHO THEY ARE. TRUST ME, I'VE SPENT TIME WITH THE PEOPLE BEHIND MARINUS.

HOW LONG TILL THEY LOCATE OUR ORBIT?

DEPENDS ON THEIR FIRE RATE AND EXACTLY WHAT KIND OF MISSILES THEY'RE USING--

--BUT NOT LONG. UNDER 36 HOURS.

GET EVERYONE IN HERE. SAMANTHA, MARKS--

--ANYONE WHO'S WORKING ON ANYTHING THAT COULD HELP.

HYDE, GO KEEP EVERYONE CALM. JUST EXPLAIN THE SITUATION AND--

--NO. I'M STAYING RIGHT HERE. I WANT TO BE A PART OF THIS.

I DIDN'T GET MYSELF OUT OF THAT CELL JUST TO BE RELEGATED TO SOME BACK CORNER.

FINE, FINE. WHATEVER. JUST GET PEOPLE IN HERE. NOW.

"IDEAS?"

WE CAN SYNTHESIZE A PROPELLANT, SHOOT THE MISSILES DOWN BEFORE THEY HIT US.

BUT WE'D NEED MORE THAN JUST PROPELLANT.

WE CAN INTERPOLATE TRAJECTORY DATA--

THAT MUCH DATA? MY TEAM IS GOOD, BUT ONE SCREW-UP AND WE'D BE DONE FOR.

WE SHOULD BUILD THE SYSTEM NOW. WE CAN USE AN ITERATIVE PROCESS FOR TARGETING--

I DON'T KNOW--

THAT'S A LOT OF UNKNOWN ELEMENTS TO TOSS AT OUR ALREADY TENUOUS POSITION.

WELL, GO FIGURE IT OUT, SAM. THIS IS WHAT WE'RE DOING!

IT CAN--

IT FEELS SAFE TO ME--

IF IT KEEPS US ALIVE--

HOLD ON, HYDE. SHE SAID IT'S DANGEROUS--

I DON'T THINK THIS IS THE BEST IDEA.

IT'S DANGEROUS, BUT WE DON'T HAVE TIME FOR ANYTHING ELSE! I DON'T PARTICULARLY WANT TO BECOME A SPACE-AGE MARTYR--

NEITHER DO I!

ANOTHER LAUNCH--FROM CENTRAL ASIA. IT'S NOT ON A COLLISION COURSE BUT, MAN... THEY'RE GETTING CLOSER.

IF WE SUCCESSFULLY SHOOT DOWN EVERY ONE OF THEIR MISSILES, THAT'S JUST A DRAW. I DON'T WANT A DRAW.

I WANT A WIN.

I WANT SOMETHING VITROS WOULD DO. SOMETHING NEW.

THE WIN IS THAT WE SURVIVE.

AND WHAT IF ONE OF THE DETONATIONS BOMBARDS US WITH RADIATION? WHAT THEN?

MY SOLUTION-- *OUR* SOLUTION-- IS SIMPLE. IT'S EXPEDIENT. IT'S EFFECTIVE.

AND WE NEED TO IMPLEMENT IT NOW--

THE WAY I SEE IT, THEY AREN'T LAUNCHING MISSILES AT US. THEY'RE LAUNCHING RAW MATERIALS.

ALL WE HAVE TO DO IS TAKE THEM.

WHAT ABOUT SOME KIND OF A SHIELD SYSTEM?

ELECTROMAGNETICS-- HMMMM--HUGE ENERGY OUTPUT-- SURE--MAYBE WE COULD POLARIZE OPPOSITE ENDS OF OUR HULL AND CREATE A KIND OF NET--BUT--

UH-- I DON'T KNOW--

I LIKE THE THOUGHT, BUT HYDE IS RIGHT. WE'RE RUNNING OUT OF TIME HERE!

YOU'RE TALKING ABOUT A SYSTEM WE WOULDN'T BE ABLE TO TEST OR IMPLEMENT TILL A MISSILE WAS ABOUT TO HIT US--

IT'S IN MOMENTS LIKE THIS THAT WE FIND OUT WHO WE REALLY ARE. WHO ARE WE, MARKS?

WE HAVE TO TRY TO THINK OF SOMETHING BETTER THAN JUST "BLOW IT UP BEFORE IT BLOWS US UP!"

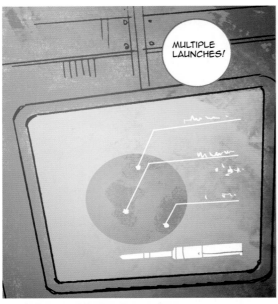

MULTIPLE LAUNCHES!

LILA, DON'T DISMISS THE PROPELLANT IDEA JUST BECAUSE IT'S MINE.

BUT I ALSO JUST FREED US FROM MARINUS. AND I CAN SOLVE THIS PROBLEM.

WHAT DID YOU JUST SAY?

YOU FEEL THREATENED BY MY ROLE AS LEADER. IT'S OBVIOUS. JUST DON'T LET IT GET US ALL KILLED.

THAT IS IT!

I TRIED TO GIVE YOU THE BENEFIT OF THE DOUBT, HYDE. I REALLY DID. BUT NO MORE.

I KNOW WHAT YOU GAVE TO MARINUS.

I SAW IT IN THEIR FILES.

YOU DID WORSE THAN JUST GET US ALL BLASTED INTO SPACE. YOU *BETRAYED* US.

C'MON, LILA--

EVERYTHING WE'VE BEEN DOING UP HERE, ALL OF THE INNOVATION, ALL OF THE WORK-- HE SOLD IT ALL TO MARINUS.

THAT WAS HIS DEAL WITH THEM.

HE GATHERS US ALL TOGETHER. MARINUS GIVES US A PLACE OF OUR OWN-- BUT EVERYTHING WE DO THERE IS GIVEN TO THEM. TO EXPLOIT. TO USE.

THE WHOLE STATION WAS LITTERED WITH TRANSMITTERS-- TINY LITTLE LEAKS- DRIPPING OUR WORK BACK TO THEM.

LILA, NO WAY.

I DIDN'T WANT TO BELIEVE IT, BUT READ BETWEEN THE LINES OF ANY TECH INNOVATION--

AND YOU'LL SEE THEY'VE BEEN USING OUR TECH. USING US.

LOOK-- ARTIFICIAL GRAVITY USED IN NEW DESIGNS--

LOOK HERE. HYDROPONIC TECHNIQUES TOO SIMILAR TO OURS TO BE COINCIDENCE--

YOU HAVE TO THINK BACK ON THOSE MOMENTS. IT WAS LIFE OR DEATH! I HAD TO DO WHAT WOULD SAVE US--

WHAT WAS EXPEDIENT. OUR BRAINS--OUR INTELLIGENCE-- THEY WERE THE ONLY BARGAINING CHIPS I HAD.

THERE WAS NO TIME FOR ANYTHING ELSE? IT WAS THE "EXPEDIENT" SOLUTION!?

DID YOU EVEN STOP TO THINK ABOUT IT? DO YOU EVER?

IT WASN'T AN EASY DECISION --BUT IT WAS THAT OR DEATH THAT--

WHACK

AMAZING. OUR LIVES COULD END AT ANY MOMENT AND THE TWO ALPHA MALES ARE FIGHTING LIKE ANIMALS.

YOU'D THINK WE'D HAVE BETTER-DEVELOPED SURVIVAL INSTINCTS.

I DON'T SEE YOU HELPING.

STOP IT!

THERE. NOW LET'S FIGURE THIS OUT BEFORE WE ALL GET BLOWN TO PIECES--

GOOD, THANK YOU. NOW IF YOU'LL KINDLY ESCORT YOUR MAN-APE OUT OF HERE-- AND NEXT TIME KEEP YOUR MOUTH SHUT--

THUNK

GETTING CLOSER--

ENOUGH!

THIS ISN'T THE PLAYGROUND! QUIT SQUABBLING LIKE CHILDREN--

HYDE, YOU DON'T DESERVE TO CALL YOURSELF A VITRO FOR WHAT YOU DID--

AND LILA--

FOR MONTHS NOW I'VE WATCHED YOU MARCH AROUND HERE PRETENDING TO BE IN CHARGE--

NO MORE. NO ONE IS IN CHARGE OF US FROM NOW ON. NO LEADERS, ONLY VITROS.

GET THEM OUT OF HERE.

NO!

DON'T DO THIS, MARKS!

"NO LEADERS, ONLY VITROS." WHERE THE HELL DID THAT COME FROM?

I HAVE NO IDEA.

DIDN'T THINK YOU HAD IT IN YOU.

I DON'T WANT TO DIE TODAY. SO WHAT CAN WE DO?

ALL THE PREVIOUS OPTIONS ARE VIABLE--NONE OF THEM ARE IDEAL.

WHAT ABOUT A PROPULSION SYSTEM FOR US? WE COULD DODGE THE MISSILES--

IMPOSSIBLE. TOO MUCH ENERGY REQUIRED. WHAT IF WE DROPPED SOME KIND OF COUNTERMEASURE? A CAMOUFLAGE?

MADE OF WHAT?

LILA WAS RIGHT ABOUT ONE THING: IF WE COULD CAPTURE THOSE MISSILES-- STEAL THEM-- MAKE THEM OURS.

WE'D BE A FORCE THEN.

THERE'S ONE THING WE MIGHT TRY.

ARE YOU GOING TO KICK US OUT OF HERE TOO?

NOT AT THIS EXACT INSTANT, NO.

TELL US WHAT THAT THING DOES.

IT'S LIKE A TOY THAT ADJUSTS WITH GRAVITY-WELL DISPLACEMENTS AND DENSITIES--

YOU SEE, WE ARTIFICIALLY INCREASE THE DENSITY OF THIS OBJECT HERE, CREATING A SEVERE GRAVITY WELL AROUND IT-- IT'S FUN.

COULD YOU DO THAT ON A LARGER SCALE?

SURE.

WE CAN DO THIS?

WE CAN DO THIS.

IF WE DO IT RIGHT, THE MISSILES WILL BE PUT INTO AN ORBIT AROUND THE SHIP--

WHAT ABOUT THEIR FIRING MECHANISMS?

SIMPLE ENOUGH. WE JUST BLOCK THE SIGNAL.

THEN WE SEND OUT A RELAY TEAM AND DISMANTLE THEM LIKE SATELLITES--

VERY, VERY DANGEROU SATELLITES

YOU TWO, COME WITH ME.

WE'RE GOING TO HEAD DOWN INTO THE POWER CORES--

I'LL GATHER MY TEAM. WE'LL BE READY FOR IMPLEMENTATION.

HOW LONG DO WE HAVE?

NOT LONG.

THAT'S ALL RIGHT. IT NEVER IS.

INSTALL THE ROUTERS INTO PANELS A, C, AND E--

LEAVE THE INTERMEDIATE PANELS EMPTY. WE MIGHT NEED BLOWERS IN THERE--

YOU'LL NEED A CIRCULATORY SYSTEM HERE, FOR COOLANT. OTHERWISE IT'LL BE FIRE CITY ALL OVER THIS DECK.

AND MAKE SURE YOU DON'T OVERCHARGE THIS BOARD HERE OR WE MIGHT END UP BEING CRUSHED IN OUR OWN GRAVITY WELL.

ANYTHING?

NOT YET.

"OUR LUCK'S GOING TO RUN OUT ANY MOMENT."

TELL ME THAT THING IS ALMOST READY.

NOT YET-- GOING TO BE AT LEAST ANOTHER HOUR--

WE HAVE A LAUNCH!

IT'S ON INTERCEPT COURSE. THEY'VE GOT US.

SON OF A BITCH--

ALL RIGHT, LISTEN UP!

A MISSILE JUST LAUNCHED ON A COLLISION COURSE WITH US. WE HAVE UNDER AN HOUR TO MAKE THIS WORK.

WE CAN STILL DO IT.

IT DOESN'T NEED TO BE PERFECT. IT JUST NEEDS TO KEEP US ALIVE.

JUST NEEDS TO KEEP US ALIVE.

WE'VE GOT IMPACT IN T-MINUS TEN AND COUNTING.

MARKS--

I HEAR YOU! IT'S HOOKED UP--

I'M ON MY WAY TO CONNECT IT.

"T-MINUS FIVE, MARKS!"

CONNECTING IT--

IT'S ON-- HIT IT!

I WISH I KNEW HOW TO PRAY--THIS WOULD BE A GOOD TIME.

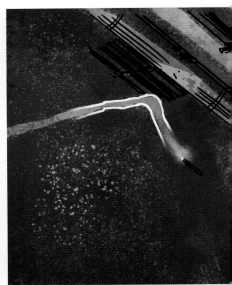

IT'S WORKING.

MISSILE IS IN A SECURE ORBIT.

DETONATION IS DISARMED.

STILL ALIVE.

READING MULTIPLE LAUNCHES INBOUND.

THREE FROM US SITES. FOUR FROM THE TURKISH QUADRANT--

THE WHOLE BOARD IS LIGHTING UP!

THEY KNOW WE'VE GOT DEFENSES UP.

BUT I DON'T THINK THEY REALIZE THAT EVERY MISSILE THEY SEND UP NOW IS JUST GOING TO BECOME OURS.

THEY'RE DESPERATE--

THAT'S NOT DESPERATION. IT'S FEAR.

"A BUNCH OF KIDS WHO HATE THEM JUST BECAME A NUCLEAR POWER."

THE END

## NEXUS OMNIBUS VOLUME 1

*Steve Rude and Mike Baron*
A multiple Eisner Award–winning series that defined the careers of acclaimed creators Steve Rude and Mike Baron, *Nexus* is a modern classic. In 2841 Nexus, a godlike figure, acts as judge, jury, and executioner for the vile criminals who appear in his dreams. He claims to kill in self-defense, but why? Where do the visions come from, and where did he get his powers?

ISBN 978-1-61655-034-9 | $24.99

## STAR WARS OMNIBUS: BOBA FETT

*Thomas Andrews, Mike Kennedy, Ron Marz, John Ostrander, Ian Gibson, Cam Kennedy, and Francisco Ruiz Velasco*
Boba Fett, the most feared, most respected, and most loved bounty hunter in the galaxy, now has all of his comics stories collected into one massive volume! There's no job too deadly for the man in Mandalorian armor!

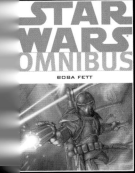

ISBN 978-1-59582-418-9 | $24.99

## MASS EFFECT VOLUME 1: REDEMPTION

*Mac Walters, John Jackson Miller, and Omar Francia*
Collecting the four-issue miniseries, *Mass Effect* Volume 1 features essential developments in the *Mass Effect* gaming saga, plus a special behind-the-scenes section with sketches and more.

ISBN 978-1-59582-481-3 | $16.99

## DARK MATTER VOLUME 1: REBIRTH

*Joseph Mallozzi, Paul Mullie, and Garry Brown*
Sci-fi action from the writers of *Stargate SG-1*! The crew of a derelict spaceship awakens from stasis in the farthest reaches of space. With no recollection of who they are or how they got on board, their only clue is a cargo bay full of weaponry and a destination that is about to become a war zone!

ISBN 978-1-59582-998-6 | $14.99

# FROM DARK HORSE BOOKS

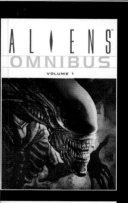

### ALIENS OMNIBUS VOLUME 1

*Mark Verheiden, Mark Nelson, Sam Kieth, and Den Beauvais*
Dark Horse Comics took the industry by storm with its release of *Aliens*, a comics series
that for the first time captured the power of film source material and expanded its universe
in a way that fans applauded worldwide. Now, the first three Dark Horse *Aliens* series are
collected in a value-priced, quality-format omnibus, featuring nearly four hundred story pages
in full color.

ISBN 978-1-59307-727-3 | $24.99

### PREDATOR OMNIBUS VOLUME 1

*Mark Verheiden, Dan Barry, Chris Warner, Ron Randall, and others*
Trophy hunters from another world, hiding in plain sight, drawn to heat and conflict. A historical
scourge, lethal specters, powerful, savage, merciless. Utilizing their feral instincts and
otherworldly technology in the sole pursuit of the most dangerous game . . . Man.

ISBN 978-1-59307-732-7 | $24.99

### TERMINATOR OMNIBUS VOLUME 1

*James Robinson, John Arcudi, Ian Edginton, Chris Warner, and others*
Terminators—indestructible killing engines hiding inside shells of flesh and blood. Tireless,
fearless, merciless, unencumbered by human emotion, dedicated to the complete eradication
of mankind. *The Terminator* is one of the finest examples of bringing top comics talents to the
expansion of a premier action/adventure mythos.

ISBN 978-1-59307-916-1 | $24.99

### ALIEN LEGION OMNIBUS VOLUME 1

*Alan Zelenetz, Frank Cirocco, Chris Warner, Terry Shoemaker, Terry Austin,
and Randy Emberlin*
Footsloggers and soldiers of fortune, priests, poets, killers, and cads—they fight for a future
Galarchy, for cash, for a cause, for the thrill of adventure. Culled from the forgotten and
unwanted of three galaxies, they are trained to be the most elite, and expendable, of fighting
forces. *Alien Legion Omnibus* Volume 1 features over three hundred story pages of the
groundbreaking series!

ISBN 978-1-59582-394-6 | $24.99

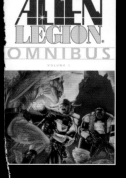

DARK HORSE BOOKS BRINGS YOU

# THE BEST IN SCIENCE FICTION!

### FEAR AGENT LIBRARY EDITION
### VOLUME 1 HC
*Rick Remender, Tony Moore, Kieron Dwyer, Francesco Francavilla, and Jerome Opeña*
When down-and-out alien exterminator Heath Huston stumbles upon an extraterrestrial plot to commit genocide against the human species, he must put down the bottle and resume his role as a peacekeeper . . . as the last fear agent.

ISBN 978-1-61655-005-9 | $49.99

### FALLING SKIES
*Paul Tobin and Juan Ferreyra*
In the heart of Boston, following the devastating events of an alien invasion, history professor Tom Mason and his sons meet up with the second Mass, a militia group determined to wipe out the aliens. But with the militia's supplies running low, Tom must locate an old friend to equip his team in order to ensure the survival of the human race!

VOLUME 1 TPB
ISBN 978-1-59582-737-1 | $9.99

VOLUME 2: THE BATTLE OF FITCHBURG TPB
ISBN 978-1-61655-014-1 | $9.99

### SERENITY VOLUME 1: THOSE LEFT BEHIND HC
*Joss Whedon, Brett Mathews, Will Conrad, Adam Hughes, and Laura Martin*
A previously unknown chapter in the lives of his favorite band of space brigands in this comics prequel of the *Serenity* feature film.

ISBN 978-1-59307-449-4 | $19.99

### SERENITY VOLUME 2: BETTER DAYS AND OTHER STORIES HC
*Joss Whedon, Patton Oswalt, Zack Whedon, Brett Matthews, Will Conrad, and others*
The crew takes on a heist that promises a big payoff. But when someone is taken captive, the gang must put aside their enduring differences and work together, at the risk of losing their cash prize.

ISBN 978-1-59582-739-5 | $14.99

### SERENITY VOLUME 3: THE SHEPHERD'S TALE HC
*Joss Whedon, Zack Whedon, and Chris Samnee*
One of *Serenity*'s greatest mysteries is finally revealed in *The Shepherd's Tale*! Who was Book before meeting Mal and the rest of the *Serenity* crew, how did he become one of their most trusted allies, and how did he find God in a bowl of soup? Answers to these and more questions about Book's past are uncovered in this rollicking, action-packed epic!

ISBN 978-1-59582-561-2 | $14.99